The Reminiscences

of

Rear Admiral George van Deurs

U. S. Navy (Retired)

Volume II

U. S. Naval Institute
Annapolis, Maryland
1974

REAR ADMIRAL GEORGE VAN DEURS
UNITED STATES NAVY, RETIRED

George Van Deurs was born in Portland, Oregon, on July 25, 1901, a son of Henry Martin Van Deurs and Mrs. (Sallie Forester Nice) Van Duers. He attended Jefferson High School in Portland prior to receiving a senatorial appointment to the United States Naval Academy, Annapolis, Maryland, in August, 1917. The next summer he served as a midshipman aboard the USS MAINE, operating with the Atlantic Fleet during World War I. He graduated and was commissioned Ensign in June, 1920 with the Class of 1921, and subsequently advanced through all the grades to attain the rank of Captain in April, 1943. He was appointed Commodore and served one year, May 1945-1946, when he reverted in rank to Captain. He transferred to the Retired List of the Navy on June 30, 1951 and was advanced to Rear Admiral on the basis of combat awards.

After graduation in 1920, he served a year in the battleship USS TENNESSEE on junior officer duties. Three months' instruction in engineering in the USS WILLIAM JONES was followed by duty from October, 1921 to June, 1923 as Chief Engineer of the USS COGHLAN, and in addition he was Executive Officer of that destroyer for the first year of that period. He then had instruction and flight training at the Naval Air Station, Pensacola, Florida, and was designated Naval Aviator #3109 on January 11, 1924. In May of that year he was assigned duty as pilot with Torpedo Squadron 1 then attached to the USS WRIGHT, tender. After seven months with that squadron he transferred to Observation Squadron 3, then being organized as the first squadron to operate regularly from catapults, based on the USS MEMPHIS. This tour included the Fleet's cruise to Australia and New Zealand in 1925, and from January to March, 1926 he was on temporary additional duty at the Naval Air Station, Coco Solo, Canal Zone.

After four months with Observation Squadron 1 in the USS WEST VIRGINIA, he served a tour of three years at the Naval Air Station, Pensacola, Florida, serving first as Flight Instructor, later as the Station Engineer Officer and Test Pilot. For his work in flood relief flying on the Mississippi River area in May, 1927, he was commended by the Secretary of the Navy and the Governor of Louisiana, and the next spring, for similar work in Alabama, he earned the thanks of the Post Office Department and a commendation from the Secretary of the Navy.

In September, 1929 he arrived on the Asiatic Station, and had three years' duty in Scouting Squadron 8 based on the tender USS JASON, with additional duty as Assembly and Repair Officer and Test Pilot of the Asiatic Station. During that period the JASON earned the Yangtze Service Medal. During the fall of 1931 he had temporary additional duty for about two months as an Aviation Observer at Singapore and in the Netherlands East Indies, and was especially commended by Commander Destroyers, Asiatic Fleet.

Returning from the Far East in June, 1932, he served three years as Erection and Test Superintendent and Test Pilot of the Naval Air Station, San Diego, California. Innovations in organization and methods originated and developed by him at this time resulted in large savings of both time and money in aircraft overhaul, and were widely adopted by other stations.

The year June, 1935-1936, he served as Flight Officer of Scouting Squadron 1, based in the USS RANGER, and for three months had additional duty as Commanding Officer of the experimental Cold Weather Test Detachment of planes aboard that ship. The accomplishments of this detachment were specially commended. Aboard the USS SARATOGA he served one year as Flight Deck Officer, and the following year he was Assistant Air Officer and Operations Officer. In June, 1938 he became Structural Overhaul Superintendent and Test Pilot at the Naval Air Station, Norfolk, Virginia.

In March, 1939 he transferred to command of Patrol Squadron 23 based at Pearl Harbor, Territory of Hawaii. Under his command the Squadron, later redesignated Patrol Squadron 11, earned commendations for all fleet exercises in which it participated, and for gunnery efficiency in the year 1939-40. He also served for a few months as Chief Staff Officer of Patrol Wing 2.

On August 29, 1941 he reported for duty as Assistant Superintendent of Aviation Training at the Naval Air Station, Corpus Christi, Texas, and later was Superintendent of Training. When Corpus Christi was organized as a Training Center, he had additional duty as Chief of Staff. During that period he was largely responsible for the reorganization and expansion occasioned by the outbreak of the war, and by spring of 1943, the Center was graduating 300 pilots per week with over 1400 officers serving in the Training department, and about 18,000 enlisted men at the Center. This was the peak of its war expansion.

In May, 1943 he was ordered to report to the Commander, Air Force, South Pacific. For services in that assignment, he was awarded the Legion of Merit and made an Honorary Commander of the Order of the British Empire by the New Zealand government. The citations follow:

Legion of Merit: "For exceptionally meritorious conduct in the performance of outstanding services to the Government of the United States as Plans Officer and subsequently as Chief of Staff for Commander Aircraft, South Pacific Force, from May 21, 1943 to April, 1944. (He) capably supervised the preparation of master plans for air operations in the New Georgia area and for the development of air bases at Vella LaVella and Treasury Islands; prepared the preliminary air plans for the occupation and development of the Empress Augusta Bay Area on Bougainville. Subsequently assuming the responsibilities of Chief of Staff, he continued to maintain high standards among all staff members and on numerous occasions capably performed the duties of Commander Aircraft, South Pacific Force, during the absence of that Commander."

Order of the British Empire (Honorary Commander): "Captain van Duers arrived in the South Pacific Area in April 1943, and became Staff Officer (Plans) to Commander Aircraft South Pacific, in which appointment he contributed materially to the successful operations in New Georgia and Bougainville. . . By his active interest in the Royal New Zealand Air Force of No. 1 Islands Group, and particularly in his advanced planning of its employment in new and forward locations, problems were considerably eased, thus facilitating the maximum operational efficiency under exceptionally difficult conditions."

Rear Admiral George Van Deurs, USN Retired

On June 15, 1944, when the original South Pacific organization was disbanded, he assumed command of the USS CHENANGO (CVE-28), which thereafter provided air support for the seizure of Morotai, Leyte, and Okinawa. For services in that command, he was awarded two Gold Stars in lieu of the second and third Legion of Merit, each with combat distinguishing device V, and the CHENANGO was awarded the Navy Unit Commendation. The citations in part follow:

"For exceptionally meritorious conduct in the performance of outstanding services . . . as Commanding Officer of an Escort Carrier Division during combat operations against enemy Japanese forces in the Pacific War Area, from October 18 to 24 and on October 28 and 29, 1944. . . . (He) expertly directed the activities of his ship and squadron in delivering vigorous aerial offensives against heavily defended enemy-held islands despite repeated attacks by hostile aircraft. . ."

Third Legion of Merit: ". . . as Commanding Officer of the USS CHENANGO, during operations against enemy Japanese forces in the vicinity of Sakishima Gunto and Okinawa on April 9, 1945. When a landing plane started a raging fire on the flight deck among parked planes loaded with bombs, rockets and .50 caliber ammunition, (he) assisted in averting disaster by expertly directing fire-fighting and bomb disposal forces and contributed materially to restoring the CHENANGO to normal operations within a few hours, thereby enabling the ship to remain in action for an additional 66 days. . ."

Navy Unit Commendation—USS CHENANGO: "For outstanding heroism in action against enemy Japanese forces in the air, ashore and afloat. . . . Attacking boldly by day and night in the face of heavy enemy resistance, the courageous officers and men of the CHENANGO achieved a notable record of service and aggressiveness in combat.. . ."

In May, 1945 he was relieved of that command and reported for duty as Chief of Staff to Commander, Battleship Squadron 1, and Commander Task Force 54, aboard the battleship TENNESSEE, almost 25 years after he served in her as Ensign. She participated in the bombardment of Okinawa until that island was secured, followed by minesweeping operations in the China Sea, and raids along the China Coast. With the task force commander, he moved into the PENNSYLVANIA about two days before VJ day. About 12 hours later, without any warning, an enemy aviator sneaked into Buckner Bay and hit her with a torpedo. The next day the staff moved back to the TENNESSEE. Service with that squadron brought him a Letter of Commendation from Commander, Fifth Fleet, and a bronze star for the Navy Unit Commendation ribbon, awarded to the USS TENNESSEE, for her "splendid record of achievements from the Aleutians to the Ryukyus. . ."

From the close of the war until December, 1945, he still participated in the operations of Commander Battleship Squadron 1 for the evacuation of prisoners from Western Japan, and the landing of occupation forces. That squadron was then decommissioned, and he became Commander Task Group 55.2 and Commander Naval Forces, Kyushu, Japan, in the cruiser OKLAHOMA CITY, and later in the ATLANTA. While on this assignment he controlled the operations of all Naval units west of Kure. In April, 1946 the last of the occupation duties in the area were turned over to forces ashore, the task group was dissolved, and he was detached and returned to the United States. Upon arrival, he was briefly attached to Fleet Air Wing 8 at Alameda, California, as Commanding Officer. The next June he was ordered to the Naval War College, Newport, Rhode Island, and completed the senior course there a year later.

On July 7, 1947 he assumed command of the carrier USS PHILIPPINE SEA at New York, New York, and during the next year the ship operated in the Atlantic and Mediterranean, winning commendations from the Commander, Sixth Fleet and the Battle Efficiency Pennant. Detached at the end of 1948, he reported to duty in the Office of the Chief of Naval Operations, Navy Department, in connection with aviation planning. In May, 1950 he joined the staff of Commander Eastern Atlantic and Mediterranean, and served one year, at that time returning to the Office of the Chief of Naval Operations. He was so attached until relieved of active duty pending his retirement on June 30, 1951.

In addition to the Legion of Merit and two Gold Stars with Combat V, the Commendation Ribbon, and the Navy Unit Commendation Ribbon with bronze star, Rear Admiral Van Deurs has the Victory Medal, Atlantic Fleet Clasp (USS MAINE); the Yangtze Service Medal (USS JASON); the American Defense Service Medal, Fleet Clasp; the American Campaign Medal; the Asiatic-Pacific Campaign Medal with silver star (five engagements); the Philippine Liberation Ribbon with one star; the World War II Victory Medal; the Navy Occupation Service Medal; and the Order of the British Empire (Honorary Commander).

In 1924 Rear Admiral Van Deurs married Miss Ann Shepard of Poley, Alabama. They have two daughters, Sally and Katherine. His official address is 118 Northwest King Avenue, Portland 10, Oregon.

He is a member of Quiet Birdmen, Los Angeles Hangar.

5 July 1951

Preface

Volume II of the reminiscences of Rear Admiral George van Deurs, U. S. Navy (Retired) takes up the story of his career in Naval Aviation at a point when he was assigned to the Naval Air Station in Norfolk (1938) and concludes with his retirement in 1951. Commander Etta Belle Kitchen, U. S. Navy (Retired) conducted the interviews in 1969 for the program of the Oral History Office, U. S. Naval Institute, Annapolis, Maryland.

Admiral van Deurs has read the transcript as made from the tapes and has made a number of corrections. The MS was re-typed and indexed for the convenience of the reader.

DECLARATION OF TRUST

The undersigned does hereby appoint and designate as his (her) Trustee herein, the Secretary-Treasurer and Publisher of the United States Naval Institute to perform and discharge the following duties, powers, and privileges in connection with the possession and use of a certain taped interview between the undersigned and the Oral History Department of the United States Naval Institute.

1. Classification of Transcript.

    (X)a. If classified OPEN, the transcript(s) may be read or the recording(s) audited by the qualified personnel upon presentation of proper credentials, as determined by the Secretary-Treasurer of the U. S. Naval Institute.

    ( )b. If classified PERMISSION REQUIRED TO CITE OR QUOTE, the user will be required to obtain permission in writing from the interviewee prior to quoting or citing from either the transcript(s) or the recording(s).

    ( )c. If classified PERMISSION REQUIRED, permission must be obtained in writing from the interviewee before the transcribed interview(s) can be examined or the tape recording(s) audited.

    ( )d. If classified CLOSED, the transcribed interview(s) and the tape recording(s) will be sealed until a time specified by the interviewee. This may be until the death of the interviewee or for any specified number of years.

2. It is expressly understood that in giving this authorization, I am in no way precluded from placing such restrictions as I may desire upon use of the interview at any time during my lifetime, nor does this authorization in any way affect my rights to the copyright of my literary expressions that may be contained in the interview.

Witness my hand and seal this 19th day of May 1970

G. van Deurs

I hereby accept and consent to the foregoing Declaration of Trust and the powers therein conferred upon me as Trustee:

R. E. Bassler Jr

We tried it again. I stood down there, and believe it or not the force was so great that this stuff came through the pores of the metal of that steel forging. They'd given us the wrong setting for the valve. If we'd ever handled an airplane that way it would have torn the tail end right off the airplane.

We horsed around with it, modified the valves to some extent, got it so it worked all right. It really made you bug-eyed, the force that gear could absorb.

Q: I wouldn't believe it possible.

van Deurs: The cylinder was a heavy steel forging, maybe an inch thick. This stuff squirted through. It just came out like perspiration all over it.

Q: Then you went back to the Naval Air Station at Norfolk.

van Deurs: I was promised a job in Washington, and then my orders came through for Norfolk. I wanted to know why, and they said - the A & R department was in a hell of a fix down there, having a lot of trouble, and they didn't have an officer with any preivous shop experience there. The number two man and the head man were postgraduate aviation engineers, engineering duty only people, and they'd been sitting in Washington writing specifications and so on, but neither of them had ever run a shop. They wanted somebody with shop experience.

I was pretty sore, because when I'd been passed over Towers said, "You ought to get out of this engineering. There are too many people think you're engineering duty only, or aeronautical PG." I'd done about ten years of test work and so on by that time. Here I was right back in it.

Q: You hadn't been promoted when you were on the SARA?

van Deurs: I had been promoted.

Q: So you did take the orders, even though you weren't happy with them?

van Deurs: Oh yes, you always took the orders. But I found myself the STructural Overhaul Officer and test pilot at Norfolk - same thing I'd done at North Island and to some extent in China, and at Pensacola.

Q: It really was a natural assignment, in that field.

van Deurs: It was natural, but I'd done too much of it.
I found that all the problems were problems I'd licked somewhere else. The answers were obvious. It was the same old routine, and they had several thousand civilian employees, and quite a few sailors in the shops, but no airplanes going out the front door. None of them ever happened to get put together again.

Q: You met the same problems you met at San Diego, didn't you?

van Deurs: It was much worse at Norfolk. It was kind of boring. I was kind of bitter about being back in the same thing.

Q: You say you were the Structural Overhaul and ..

van Deurs: And test pilot.

Q: Who was the C O?

van Deurs: Pat Bellinger commanded the Station.

But the trouble was in the shops complicated by a labor problem angle. The labor unions over in the Navy Yard had been pretty red, and caused a lot of trouble. The civilian employees at the Air Station were affiliated with these unions. There were a lot of troublemakers out in the shops. And also, a movement that was being headed up by some of the top civilian employees, to get all officers out of the overhaul business, and make it all civilian, so that there would be some top civilian jobs. So in addition to the problems of poor organization, there was a lot of active opposition. It was just not a healty situation.

Ted Longquist who was the Repair Officer, the head of the shops

Q: Was he an officer?

van Deurs: He was a lieutenant commander, engineering duty only, and scared to death of the unions, of their political pull.

They had quite a lobby in Washington and were pretty powerful with the Virginia representative, and Ted was scared to death they'd smear his record. He insisted that everything be in writing. We could not make a move without writing a memorandum to the boss. That meant hours of overtime work at night catching up with the memoranda.

Nick Draim, the number two, had been with me on the SARATOGA, but he aslo was an EDO without any shop experience. He was a lot smarter man than the head man. We used to sit at desks in the repair office facing each other. We soon learned that we couldn't speak across the desk without it being reported to the troublemakers and causing trouble.

Q: That's the people in the union, the civilians?

van Deurs: Yes. We didn't know who the spies were in the office, but we knew there were some.

Q: That's a lovely situation.

van Deuss: I'd look up and say, "Hey, Nick, suppose we do this." "Think it would be a good idea." Within an hour there'd be a delegation waiting on Bellinger, the captain of the Air Station, saying that they understood it was planned to do so and so and they objected. Longquist would get called on the map - he'd never heard of the idea - it was some chance remark between Nick and me.

It got so bad that if I wanted to say anything to Nick, I'd get up and walk out of the office, walk across the concrete over to the propeller shop, get on the telephone, call Nick, "Say, Nick, there's a propeller blade over here that I'm not sure of, I don't know if we should repair or scrap it, I'd like your advice, come on over." Hang up the phone, walk out, and I'd meet Nick in the middle of the concrete halfway and say, "No propeller problem, I just wanted to say so and so," where there was nobdy within a hundred feet of us.

Q: What a horrible working situation.

van Deurs: It was very uncomfortable. Then Nick and I got the idea of finding out who the snoops were.

We lived near each other out in Norfolk, and we'd get together of an evening over a couple of beers, and think up a couple of very wild ideas. Next morning, we'd manage to meet on the shop floor with only one other person present, somebody we kind of suspected, and we'd spring this wild idea, which we had no intention of doing there, never mention it again.

Q: He could only know it from hearing your conversation.

van Deurs: Yes. So then if there was a squawk right away quick from the captain's office, we knew that man was on the black list. If nothing happened we said, "Well, maybe he's okay."

The foreman, I guess, of the final assembly plant was an old ex-chief petty officer, a very solid citizen. He and I walked into the sheet metal plant one day where the foreman was a civilian, one of the chief troublemakers. And I knew he was a liar to boot. AndI caught him flatfooted in some kind of a lie - something that was going on. I jumped down his throat with both feet. It left him kind of shaken when we walked out of the place.

The chief said, "Gee, boss, you looked like there was fire coming out of your eyes. Dont' do that around here, you'll get sent to sea. They've all been shanghaied out of here for picking on those guys." I said, "That's all right, I want to go to sea, I don't like it here. I'll do it again, if you'll guarantee I'll go to sea."

After a couple of weeks I decided this thing was for the birds, just batting my head against the labor problem and the same old mechanical problems I'd licked before and told everybody how to fix. The answers were obvious. If I made it work I got no credit - Longquist would. And if I didn't make it work, why, I'd get blamed for all kinds of things.

So every Wednesday I got in an airplane and flew up to Washington to the old Navy Department, and sat on the corner of the detail officer's desk, and told him why I ought to go to sea. I said everybody else in my time had had command of a squadron, and I never had had, and I thought I ought to have a squadron.

Slats Sallada, class of '16, was too much of a gentleman to throw me out, just too nice a guy. Still I was bothering a busy man, knew it, and kept doing it. Finally to get rid of me he said, "If you put in a written request I'll see what I can do about it."

So I went back to Norfolk, wrote an elaborate request to go to sea, stated my reasons. I don't know whether it was Honus Wagner, the executive officer, or Pat Bellinger that hung an endorsement on it that they recommended that I be sent to sea, because I needed the command on my record, but they wanted my relief to report six months before I left, and put on a lot of impossible qualifications on him. So I went back to ...

Q: You say Bellinger was there?

van Deurs: Pat Bellinger was the skipper of the station.

Q: Did he know the situation you were faced with?

van Deurs: I think he probably did. The committee was always waiting on him. I don't know whether he knew how bad it was in the shop I don't think he did. But this went on about six months. We got out some airplanes in spite of the people and installed some of the systems we'd worked out in San Diego that helped, over a lot of opposition from the same people.

Q: Did you ever discover who the actual troublemakers were?

Van Deurs: Oh yes, we knew some of them. The ringleader of the whole thing was the top civilian of the place, a draftsman who ran the drafting room right next door to the main office.

Nick and I had sometimes talked things over there at night when we were the only people in the building, and that word got out. We finally decided this bird had the place bugged. We spent a couple of evenings tearing that office apart trying to find the microphone. We never did find it. That's why we were walking out on the concrete. But this bird, his name was Heckman, later got promoted to the Navy Department, and as far as I know he may still be there - one of the civilian jobs in the Navy Department.

He wanted to be the repair officer at Norfolk at that time, and he was the kingpin. He had people all over the shop coming to him with tales or anything he could use for ammunition. Still when any of us were around he was the most gracious, unctuous, breezy bird I ever saw. We never could hang anything on him. We couldn't prove it, but he was it.

Q: You must have had a miserable job.

van Deurs: Finally I went to Washington one day, and Sallada had my request, but told me he couldn't do anything about it on account of this endorsement. They'd promised King they wouldn't pull any officers out of the fleet till after the cruise. That wouldn't be over for two or three months, and there wasn't any relief for me, and so on.

The next Saturday Ann and I were week-ending in Washington. I went into the detail office and Sallada said, "I'm writing your orders to Honolulu."

I said, "Fine, thanks," and ran out. Just let it ride, didn't ask any questions or anything. I saw Towers in the corridor. He was Assistant Chief of the Bureau, just before they made him Chief.

Q: This was down at Main Navy in those days?

van Deurs: Yes.

Towers wanted to know what I was doing there. I told him Ann and I were up for the week-end, and he said, "Come around tomorrow afternoon and have cocktails with me and Pierre." We did. Ann started in gushing, "Oh, isn't it wonderful, George's orders are coming out to Honolulu."

Towers said, "Yeah. I had something to do with that. Sallada brought that request in for me to sign an endorsement - turning it down. I told him I wouldn't do that, after advising you to get out of engineering - to send you to sea." So again I owed that to a friend.

The minute the orders hit Norfolk the rumor was all over the shop that I was shanghaid. Somebody tipped me off that down in the workmen's head they were all saying the head man of the Machinists Union had gotten me thrown out of the shops. So I sent for this little guy. He was the foreman of the propeller shop, really a very decent guy, and he wasn't one of the real troublemakers. The metalsmiths, not the machinists, were the reds.

I said, "Now, I understand that you're getting some credit for sending me to sea. If you did, I want to thank you. I've been working very hard for some months to get those orders. If you had any hand in it, thank you very much."

He sputtered all over the place --- "God damn it, if his union was fighting somebody they did it openly, they didn't do it behind his back; he had nothing to do with it. Some of the others did." The word went around and I think maybe it did some good.

Then I got ready to check out. I went around to see the exec and get my orders endorsed, and the exec grabbed me by the hand and led me down to Bellinger's office and said, "Captain wants to talk to you." I sat down, and he wanted to know what was wrong with his air station. Well, I spent about an hour maybe telling him.

Q: Was he sincere in asking that question?

van Deurs: I didn't know, but I was just mad enough to tell him.

So I told him what was going on over in the shops, what was wrong with it, the labor trouble, that some officers were scared of political pressure.

Q: It's hard to think that as smart a man as he is, that he would not have known.

van Deurs: Longquist ran the shops. Bellinger had other things to worry about. But the output of the shop was below what it should have been, and these delegations were waiting on him periodically, to kick about it. So I told him what it looked like from my side of it. We parted amicably, and I went to Pearl Harbor.

Q: Do you think you were able in spite of the difficulties to accomplish anything at the Air Station?

van Deurs: I doubt if I accomplished too much.

There was one nice thing about it. After the war started I was down in Texas and flew a plane north, to swap planes. My main object was to stop in Washington and get some information for my boss. On the way north I stopped at Norfolk; I ran out of daylight. And I knew that Draim, who'd been the number two man, was now running the plant. This was in the middle of '42, I guess, maybe near the end of it.

So I went looking for Nick. I found him, about eight o'clock in the evening, over in the office of the shops. They were on twenty four hours shifts, and he had a perfectly clean desk. I said, "Nick, for crying out loud, we used to have papers piled up so high. How did you get rid of them?"

"Oh," he said, "the jeep does it," and pointed at a microphone sitting on his desk. "How does it work?"

"Well, you know all these troublemakers we used to have around here. When they come around with a kick I say, 'Is this important enough for me to make a record of it?' When they say 'No,' I say, 'Get out.' If they say 'Yes' I turn this switch and say, 'All right now let's have it,' and when they get through I give them an answer and I turn off the switch. There's a record of both. Then every once in a while there's a conference here, and it goes along so far and somebody says, 'Oh, but the Bureau won't let us do that,' So

I say, 'Wait a minute,' and I pick up the telephone and call the Bureau, and the jeep is listening. And I say, 'Can we do so and so on account of because?' and they say 'Yes, go right ahead and do it.' So I say, 'Thank you,' and there's a record of that. We don't need any papers."

He had made other improvements, and had been cracking the whip around there. He had airplanes coming out of the shop.

Q: Had any of this been your suggestion?

van Deurs: No. He'd used some of my tricks.

Nick was a smart man. He looked like a sleepy slow going dopey kind of a guy, but he thought awful fast, and people didn't bluff him easily. Longquist was bluffed by these people. As soon as Nick took over he cleaned house.

Q: Funny how individual personalities can change situations.

van Deurs: Oh, the place had expanded. It was two or three times as big as it had been two or three years before when I was there. Nick had it running like a Swiss watch.

Q: That must have been satisfying.

van Deurs: It was. I was very glad to see that. I was very glad to see Nick doing it, but that was the end of Norfolk as far as I was concerned.

There was one hangover - a couple of years later at Pearl Harbor, Admiral Fitch called me one day and said, "Turn your squadron over to the executive officer and come up here and sit down on the staff, pick some guys to help you, because the LURLINE comes in Thursday with Pat Bellinger on it and I'm leaving on Friday. I'm taking my staff with me, and Bellinger's staff won't get here for a month or so, so you're got to pick up a scratch staff and keep the wing going."

Q: This was on your next duty.

van Deurs: Yes, this was at Pearl Harbor.

I said, "I don't think Pat Bellinger's going to want me. Last time I saw him I spent an hour telling him what was wrong with his air station." Fitch said, "Never mind that, you'll do, you'll take it."

Well, it worked out that way. The tough part of it was that after a certain length of time Bellinger's staff showed up, and I was officially relieved to go back to the squadron, but from then on until I left Pearl I was always being called back up for trick jobs or trick advice for the staff. He leaned on me a bit thereafter. So I don't know, maybe it did some good to tell him the truth about his air station.

Q: I would think so.

Then when you finished your duty there, did you have any leave?

van Deurs: We had enough leave to drive to the West Coast and catch the LURLINE from San Francisco, got there early in May, 1938.

That was a rather surprising arrival. The old Hawaiian custom of aloha, welcome, and so on, and all the officers of the squadron were down at the dock. The bird I was relieving, Bob Hickey, a classmate of mine, "Where are your orders? Here, give 'em to Joe. He'll take them out and get them endorsed for you."

Q: This was the first time you'd actually been a commanding officer, wasn't it?

van Deurs: Except for the time on the RANGER.

Then, "Where do you want to live? There's a set of quarters for you out at Ford Island. If you want to wait till your furniture and stuff gets here before you move in, we can get you an apartment out at the beach."

We thought an apartment on the beach for a month would be kind of fun, so they loaded us in a car, and some of them took us out to the beach and arranged for an apartment. Somebody else brought out bags along to throw in. And, "There'll be a cocktail party in a couple of hours, we'll be back and pick you up." I said, "I'll have to check in." Bob said, "Today, we have fun."

So they took us to a cocktail party, and to dinner, and something else after that, long into the evening. Then somebody said, "Now, you don't mind if Joe here comes by at two o'clock in the morning and picks you up to take you out to the station, because the squadron's got to take-ff at three for French Frigate Shoals."

Q: Oh my, and you hadn't even logged in yet.

van Deurs: I'd sent my orders out to log in.

They said, "It was postponed so you could take part in it. It has to go right now because the moon's right. We want to try some lunar navigation on the way. So if you don't mind we'll pick you up at two o'clock."

Well, it was the first time I ever got into a PBY airplane, still pitch black, somewhere around two-thirty in the morning, first time I'd been on Ford Island."

Q: And you were commander of the whole squadron?

van Deurs: I was about to be, but we had an overlap of a couple of weeks.

Bob said, "I put you in Paul Ramsey's plane because his plane has the best cook, so when we go on these expeditions," ----
The PBY had a very nice little galley on it. To be a plane captain you had to be able to cook. That was one of the qualifications. "Gee, we'll have swell chow at breakfast on the way out and swell lunch on the way back," and so on.

We took off, flew and flew, and I kept wandering around. I began to get hungry after we'd been in the air for an hour or so. Nobody was making any move towards cooking any chow; nothing happened. I didn't know any of these people; I'd just met them the night before I didn't want to say much, but I kept getting hungrier and hungrier.

I think somebody finally made some coffee and passed that around, but that was all. I was wondering about this swell breakfast we were supposed to have.

The expedition was to rendevouz with a submarine off French Frigate Shoals, and take gasoline and supplies from it. This was practiced for a couple of years there before the war.

Q: How far was it?

van Deurs: Oh, about five hundred miles. We used to go out there so that it wouldn't be observed by the Japanese or any of their spies. We thought we'd invented something secret.

We got out there, and when our turn came we taxied up behind the NARWAHL, or NAUTILUS, whichever it was, and took a line.

Then Ramsey stood up and yelled over to the submarine to ask if they had any pots or pans they could loan us. Our crew had brought along the chow, but they'd forgotten the cooking utensils. The sub passed over a frying pan and a stew pan or something, and from then on we ate all the way back. But Paul was very much embarrassed, after boasting about his cook.

As far as the experiment went there was nothing to it. The sub passed over a hose and pumped the gasoline, and that was that. Actually I don't believe we ever used it during the war, but the Japanese did.

You mentioned a while ago the planes that flew over Pearl Harbor after December 7th ...

Q: I think it was February, '42.

van Deurs: They were seaplanes that had come from the Marshalls and refueled at French Frigate Shoals, the same place, from a Japanese submarine, and then flown over Pearl. Before the Battle of Midway, there were some more of those planes that were supposed to make that jump and make sure where our fleet was and where the carriers were - maybe that came out in the broken code. Anyway, when that submarine got to French Frigate Shoals there were a couple of American ships sitting there.

Q: Seaplanes?

van Deurs: No, ships anchored there, surface ships.

The sub radioed back to Japan, watched the ships for a couple of days, radioed back, and the flights were cancelled. It's one of the reasons our carriers got out of Pearl Harbor unobserved, to Midwa It always seemed ironical because we thought we had something very secret, and they had the same idea. Maybe they got it from us.

That was my introduction to Pearl.

Q: And whom did you relieve?

van Deurs: Bob Hickey.

They had a very nice schedule going there at Pearl Harbor in those days. We went to work at seven o'clock in the moring and quit at one. Everybody went out to shoot golf and so on. Flying was pleasant. It was very much the time of one's life. But this was in May of '38 ...

Q: '38 or '39? You were in Norfolk in '38.

van Deurs: '39, it was '39.

But before I left Norfolk I knew darn well there was going to be a war in Europe. It was very obvious that Hitler was going to force things very soon. And I assumed, since every time there'd been a big war in Europe we'd gotten sucked into it, that we'd get sucked into this one sooner or later.

So when I finally did relieve Bob a few weeks later, I started in trying to get ready for it. I called my officers in, and I think I kind of shocked them. Everybody was screaming in those days about engineering competition and communication competition and gunnery competition, everybody was reading the fine print in the books to find ways to kind of skim the rules to increase the score, and I informed them I wasn't at all interested in the scores we made on any of those competitions. I wanted them to learn how to communicate and how to shoot, and how to do the type of flying we needed to do, so that I'd feel comfortable if I was in the front seat with a couple of gunners in the back when an enemy was after us. I figured if we did that we'd get a good enough score so that we wouldn't get investigated, and that was all I cared about. I wasn't interested in the competition.

A couple of the smart boys that were real good at the fine print business didn't believe it at first. I knocked a couple of heads together and they finally got convinced that we had to get war ready in a serious way. And I was rather pleased to find that instead of trying to get off a few minutes early and get out on the golf course, these people began to stick around a little bit later with an idea to do this or that. They took my idea seriously. Some of the other squadrons pooh-poohed them and insisted that we were nuts, but I kept after the thing.

Q: What kind of thing did they stick around to do? What did you do differently than the others?

van Deurs: If you rig it this way or that way — should we do this or should we do that? It was a bunch of minor things. The main thing was that instead of trying to figure out how to get something on the towed sleeve, how to get a little bit closer, or a little bit steadier angle, or something —"I'm going to have to shoot at an airplane in the sky."

Q: They really only needed the kind of leadership you gave them.

van Deurs: Yes, they all fell into it.
Same way you had to drop a certain number of bombs every month and that was scored. We got to taking that pretty seriously, and not trying to fudge on altitutes or places or anything else, but let's put them in the barrel.

Then every once in a while some idea would come up that would mean a change in something.

Whiting was commanding the wing when I first went out there, but about the time I relieved Hickey, Bristol relieved Whiting. That was the third or fourth time I'd been with Bristol, so that when I got an idea I wanted to try something different, I had no compunction about going up to the front office and talking it over with him, and asking for permission, and getting it every time. He backed me up beautifully.

A bit later Fitch came along and relieved him, and I had sort of the same co-operation with the wing office then too. It got embarrassing in a couple of cases.

I've forgotten the exact instance now, but maybe it was some night flying or some darned thing that I decided we ought to know how to do, and I went up and asked permission to start training my people to do it. The answer was, "Gee, they all ought to know how to do that. We'll start all the squadrons doing it."

So the staff operations officer put out an order. One of my classmates had come along and taken over one of the squadrons, and he'd come to me and say, "Hey, man, you've got influence in the front office. I understand they're going to tell us to go do so and so." It was my idea. He didn't know it. I said, "I'd heard that. I thought it was a good idea."

He said, "Oh, somebody might get hurt, that might be dangerous." "Yeah, but if a war came along don't you think we ought to be able to do it?"

"Oh yeah, but gee whiz let's not do it now. Let's put it off. Let somebody else do that. I don't want trouble on my record."

He had fixed it up to command a squadron for one year, get it on his record, and then go as navigator to the SARATOGA, and ...

Q: Who was that?

van Deurs: It was a classmate of mine. He was scared to death somebody'd break an airplane or something, and he'd be blamed for it. Regularly of course I refused to intercede.

Q: Since it was your idea in the first place.

van Deurs: Usually it was my idea in the first place, but there were a lot of interesting things that came out of it.

For instance, one war problem - they wanted us to run a long patrol out of Johnston Island. At that time they only had about four thousand feet in the lagoon clear of coral. They'd blasted the coral heads out enough so you could take-off, and marked it out with buoys. To take off with a load of bombs and a full load of gasoline for a long patrol, the Catalina needed a lot more than that four thousand feet. Somewhere I had read of making circular take-offs, and decided to try it. We tried it first at Ford Island at Pearl Harbor --- started taxiing downwind, got it on the step - it would go fast enough to get it on the step - run it right down to the cane fields, then make a one hundred eighty degree turn, keeping it on the step, and take-off. The way we did it ...

Q: Did it work?

van Deurs: Yes. The two pilots had to work on the thing together. On the step there was enough control in the ailerons so that you could keep the wings level without either of the wing tips' pontoons touching the water. The second pilot handled the throttles. He'd give it full power, and as soon as it was on the step he'd throttle down a little bit. We'd get down to the end, kick hard rudder, and by working the ailerons keep level. By the time we would straighten out into the wind he'd have the engines wide open. We got so that we could start from the squadron runway, which was well down at the end of Ford Island, go down to the cane field, turn around, and be in the air before we got back to the runway.

Q: How many feet would that be?

van Deurs: Oh, I don't know. It was fairly short. It wasn't with a fullload to start out with; we tried it light.

Q: You were able to do that then?

van Deurs: The whole squadron practiced the trick then — there at Pearl Harbor. That was one of the things that my friend objected to as dangerous, but we managed to take full loads out of Johnston, which surprised some of the people on the opposition side of that war game. They thought we couldn't do it.

Q: What was the object of the war game then?

van Deurs: Oh, I don't know. We were scouting there, doing some kind of a search.

That was one of those little tricks ...

Q: Had anyone ever done it before?

van Deurs: Not that I know of. But my team was good enough so that I'd left before it happened, on 8 December, '41 they were scheduled to fly to Wake Island, to operate from Wake. The morning of the 7th the planes were all gassed up, loaded with bombs and spare parts and everything else for the move. We had moved over to Kaneohe before I left. Apparently the Japs had the word; those planes were the first thing hit. They burned up the squadron on the runway. But as soon as the smoke cleared away, Bellinger gathered up the bits and pieces of PBYs, put together all that would fly, gave them to my team, and sent them to the South Pacific. They were the first PBY squadron to move out after the attack. So the training did some good, though I wasn't there to profit by it.

Q: How far did your squadrons go from Pearl -- that was Patrol Squadron 23. How far out would you go? What was your daily mission to fly out a certain distance?

van Deurs: For a search - if we thought there was a possibility of the Japs coming or something and they threw a search around the island, we'd fly about a fourteen hour patrol.

Q: How far?

van Deurs: They flew about one hundred twenty knots, so fourteen hours - probably six half hours out, pretty near seven hundred miles out, and a cross leg, and seven hundred back, somewhere between six and seven hundred miles.

But in that squadron we flew all over the Pacific. They were building bases at Johnston and Midway and Wake, and periodically the contractor would get hard up for a part of something, and somebody would be told off to take it out. We used Midway and Johnston long before they were in commission. We flew to Canton Island, when Pan-American opened their first hotel there. They had blasted a runway out of the coral in the lagoon there. We flew some runs down there to get familiar with the place.

Q: I see. It was during this period that Pan-Am made their first flights from San Francisco or Los Angeles to Pearl, wasn't it, '39?

van Deurs: No, they were flying to Pearl and on to Manila at that time. They started to Australia during that period.

They had a little hotel on Midway. Before we had an air station there we used to use their little hotel, when we'd fly out there.

Q: Did you have any feeling when you were out there of the imminence of the Japanese attack? You left in '41.

van Deurs: Oh, very much so.

About October of '40, the Admiral came back from CinCPac one day, called in the squadron commanders and said he didn't know what it was about, but he was shown a secret message over at the Admiral's to the effect that the Japanese Fleet had disappeared and intelligence didn't know where they were.

Admiral Richardson wanted a three hundred sixty degree search around Pearl Harbor, and to keep it up - get going. All of us started out. Well, using all the planes that were at Pearl Harbor you could just make a three hundred sixty degree coverage out about six or seven hundred miles, which really wasn't far enough because you'd be at the outer limit around noon, and a carrier that was just out of sight over the horizon could start a run-in right then and be at launching point by daylight the next morning.

Q: They could follow you right in.

van Deurs: As it were, yes, but it was the best we could do.

But after about three days of that every engine in the wing needed an overhaul or a check, and every flight crew was completely exhausted. They'd flown three fourteen hour patrols in three days. And the same men had to check the engines; we had no spare mechanics. So after three days everything was grounded and we reported to the CinC that we couldn't do any more.

Then we got ordered to knock the search off, train some spare crews right away so you can keep going longer.

Well, fine, we'd go back to training, but we had no people to train for spare crews, not any spare pilots, or any spare mechanics out there.

Q: Or any machines?

van Deurs: We could fix the machines. If we had spare mechanics we could have done that work at night, but we didn't.

That happened several times between October '40 and the actual attack. I don't know how many times, but several times we were pulled out the same way. Each time it ended up, "Go back to training and train some spares," but we didn't have any.

After Kimmel took over, I know that he asked for more planes and more crews, and I saw a reply that came I think right from the White House that said that the war wasn't going to start in the Pacific, it was going to start in the Atlantic, and they were fixing up the Atlantic bases, and after they got filled up Pearl Harbor would get some more.

Q: This came from the White House?

van Deurs: Yes. It was the answer to Kimmel's request for planes and spare people.

Q: Were there no more planes there December 7th than when you were there?

van Deurs: Not a plane; the situation hadn't changed at all.

About maybe February of '41, the Commander in Chief appointed a lot of committees to consider the different aspects of the defense of Pearl Harbor. I was put on one representing the patrol wings. The Air Station sent Harry Carlson, and Halsey sent Miles Browning as the carrier man - he was Halsey's intelligence officer at the time. The Air Force sent Colonel Street, and the Coast Artillery - which manned all the anti-aircraft guns - sent another Colonel. The problem was to devise a way that planes could get in and out of Oahu without getting shot down, in case of war, and also what Air would do what and who would command what Air in case of a surprise attack.

Miles Browning was a man with a very violent temper and a very sharp mind. He was later Halsey's operations officer. And he probably was the brains behind all the early carrier raids. He'd been a squadron commander on the RANGER when I was there, and lived next door to me at Pensacola when he came there to take training when I was an instructor.

I'd seen Miles blow his top. He could be a horribly violent short-tempered man. I thought, this was going to be fun. He was the senior man on this committee.

Miles said, "Now, look, we'll hold all the meetings over at Hickam Field, " the Air Corps main field, "to pacify the Army."

While we were meeting Miles held himself in check beautifully. We'd go over there and talk all morning. The Air Force man, Colonel Street, had been through the Naval War College and thought more or less along the lines we did. What we proposed was - that there were frequently carrier squadrons on the field at Ford Island - in case of a surprise attack any fighters the Navy had on the beach would be immediately placed under the command of the Army Fighter Command. And the same way if they had any long-range bombers that could reach out where the attack was coming from - that they would be put under the command of the Patrol Wing to help the Navy Catalinas, the long-range seaplanes. That seemed pretty reasonable to everybody. So we told the yeoman to write that up, we'd meet again tomorrow morning.

The next morning Colonel Street would take back everything he'd said the day before, "Well, the Air Force can't quite agree to that, it wanted to change a lot of ifs, excepts, and buts," and so on.

"But that's the word for word what you agreed to yesterday."

"Yes, but ...

It turned out he had to go every afternoon and tell his boss, the General, what we'd agreed to, and he'd catch hell and be told to go take it back and start over again. That went on for, I don't know, several weeks. Each time, I was amazed at the way Miles Browning played ROBERTS RULES OF ORDER and looked very calm and so on, but the minute we got out of the place and got in the car to go back to the dock and the boat over to Ford Island, Miles would start cussing. And he'd cuss a blue streak from the time he got in that car until he had landed on Ford Island. He'd hold it in beautifully, but then just blow like a fire siren all the way home.

Finally we came up against the deadline. Admiral Block, the District Commandant, was ordered to collect the reports of all these committees. Miles said, "We'll write the report this way," and Bill Street said, "I'll have to put in a minority report because that's what the boss says." The other Army man was with us. So that's the way it went in - a split report.

Block wouldn't do anything about a split report, so Kimmel sent for Bellinger - told Pat to get down to Fort Shafter and talk to this Army Air General - I forget his name, I think it was Smith or Martin and see if they couldn't agree to something on this command propositi

Bellinger sent for me and said, "You've been in on this from the start, come along." So for a couple of weeks, I guess, two or three times a week, we'd ride down to Fort Shafter and chitchat with this General and his Chief of Staff - never could tune the guy down.

"Well, according to the principle of paramount interest, according to the principle of this, and the principle of that, the Air Forc believes in the principle of so and so ...." And it got so I wouldn' even listen, it was like a cracked record on a phonograph.

He was spouting principles across the desk at Pat one day; I was standing looking out the window. The Chief of Staff, man named Ryan, said, "You know, this would make a swell joint exercise, but the trouble is we haven't got time for a joint problem. We've got so much training to do. None of our bomber pilots can go out of sight of land. None of them know how to navigate. We're having an awful training problem. We just haven't got time to get mixed up with a joint exercise."

I said, "We're not talking about a joint exercise. We don't care if you never test this thing out. We're talking about who does what when the whistle blows." "Oh," he said, "you know it couldn't happen." I said, "Why not?"

He said, "Before the Japanese Fleet could ever get across the Pacific ONI would let us know. We'd have two weeks to get ready and decide what we're going to do."

I said, "Colonel, you're very flattering, but I happen to know that ONI can't guarantee that. When a ship goes to sea nobody knows where it's going. If you've been reading the newspapers you'll notice that several weeks ago a task force went out of Pearl Harbor for a weeks exercise and came back minus two cruisers. The newspapers went wild guessing where they were. They kept guessing until they suddenly turned up in Sidney. That may have been done to give the Japs a little razzle-dazzle and let them wonder. The next thing they disappeared from Sidney and turned up in Manila. We can't tell if the Japs are going to head this way instead of towards China."

Oh well, they just couldn't believe it.

So I went back to the office and went around to see Miles Browning. He knew more about Japanese capabilities than anybody else I knew at the time. I said, "Miles, what have they got, and what can they do?" He said, "Well, there's this book and this one and this one. It's all there, take them."

I went home and wrote kind of a half-assed War College estimate At least it started out like one. I looked at the charts and played Jap and found there were two different ways - one starting from Japan and one starting from the Marshalls, where they could cross the Pacific without a chance in a million of being spotted by a merchant ship or anything else. From Japan they could turn about where Ernie King had turned the SARA, head south, miss our patrols if they were out, and at dawn launch right at the point where we had launched that attack two or three years before.

Q: Even if your patrols had sighted them they would have been seven hundred miles out and too late to do anything.

van Deurs: They didn't have to sight them. Japs could do it without being sighted.

Q: And even if they had?

van Deurs: I put tracks on that chart showing how they could do it, and made recommendations, which were just exactly the recommendations Miles' committee had made in the first place - to do thus and so with the fighters and carriers, carrier planes on the beach and patrol planes and bombers. Took it to Bellinger and said, "Look, I haven't mentioned principle at all. The word principle doesn't occur. Next time we go to Shafter, and the man begins talking principles, ask him to sign this. There being no principles in it, I don't think he can object. Maybe we'll get an answer that way."

And it worked out that way. He took the paper. When the General started talking principles Pat said, "Before you get into that, maybe you'd like to look over this and sign it."

So the General did, Pat did, and they sent it over to Block as their recommendations. It was filed in the safe and nothing was ever done to put it into effect.

So when the Congressional committee investigated Pearl Harbor, Bellinger and the General both dragged their copies out of the safe and said, "See, here's what we recommended." The Congressional investigation in a little footnote says that they were the only two guys out there who knew what was going to happen. That is the way it happened. I was very glad it got Pat off the hook; he was a good guy. I was always sore that the General escaped on the same basis, because he'd obstructed the work.

Q: If you had been there on Pearl Harbor, do you think that your being there would have made any different result than happened?

van Deurs: Not a bit. Not a bit, because it was all being done on orders from higher up.

Q: You would have gone out that Sunday morning?

van Deurs: They were going to take-off the next morning for Wake.

At that time, they were worrying about submarines. They were running some patrols over the fleet operating areas looking for enemy submarines, but they weren't running the long distance search. Everybody seemed to be convinced that the Japs would attack the Philippines and not Pearl Harbor.

I got some little satisfaction from a letter from the chap who had been my executive officer. He was still there when the attack came. From one of the Jap planes, shot down in the Navy Yard, they recovered the chart, and the launching point was right where I'd put it, up to the north of the islands. It was just the logical way to do it, and that's exactly what they did.

Q: You don't have the feeling that this may have been done knowingly from Washington with the idea of uniting the American people?

van Deurs: That was one theory that was put out in Kimmel's defense. I'm not sure but what there was something to it. I think there probably was.

Richardson, you know, was relieved as Commander-in-Chief because he told the President he wouldn't be responsible for the Fleet in Pearl Harbor, wanted to bring them back to the Coast. I suspect that if Roosevelt was using it as bait, he was like a lot of the admirals he didn't believe airplanes could cause much damage, and he never expected to have the whole Fleet put out of action. If the raid had just done a little damage, it would have united the country and the war. Of course, he'd been trying to push the country into war for a year.

Q: We were practically at war in the Atlantic anyway.

van Deurs: He'd had the Navy doing every un-neutral service in the Atlantic possible, and Hitler was too smart to declare war. He had every legal excuse to, but he didn't want to get caught like the Kaiser in a two front war with us on one side of it. So he refused the bait.

Q: But there was no doubt in your mind when you were out there that this was going to happen?

van Deurs: Not a bit, no. I just didn't know when.
They were pushing the Japs into a corner. They had the Japs thinking that they had to fight to survive, and I based my argument on the fact that every war they'd gotten into they'd started with a surprise attack. They'd sunk the Chinese Fleet in the Yalu River, I believe it was in '95, before they ever declared war. And they attacked the fleet in Port Arthur before they declared war on the Russians, and tactically a surprise attack is a very effective weapon. It was logical. So on that basis of their history and their ability to do it, I said they would. There were people that agreed with me, including Miles Browning, but nobody would listen. Most of them still thought that the airplane was kind of a toy.

Q: Even the fact that the Japanese destroyed all the battleships — they themselves were having the same kind of conflict. They thought the battleships were the prime target, you know.

van Deurs: Both sides still believed in the battleship, but they at least believed that the airplane could hit. They planned Pearl Harbor, and then they went down by Singapore two days later you know and got the battleship PRINCE OF WALES and the cruiser REPULSE - that kind of put a period to the argument.

One little sidelight that comes to mind — year I was in the SARATOGA as Operations Officer, my Assistant in Air Plot was John Waldron. John was half Sioux, a member of the bar in California, a naval aviator, and a very dedicated guy. Sitting there one day, our planes were away and there was nothing much happening, we were just watching the chart and got to thinking about it. I said, "John, you know, this thing is a lot of fun playing it as a war game, but I hope we don't have to do this play seriously for keeps. These planes are getting too big and they carry too much stuff, and they go too far. If we play this thing seriously, why, a lot of people are going to get badly hurt."

John said, "Gee, do you feel that?" I said, "Yeah, I'm a pacifist, I would hate to see this thing played for keeps."

He said, "It must be the damned Indian in me, but just once in my life I want to come down in a screaming dive with my sights on a live target, and my guns going for keeps. After that I don't care what happens."

You know what happened, don't you?

Q: Wasn't he the one that went out in the Battle of Coral Sea?

van Deurs: He led Torpedo Eight at the Battle of Midway.

Q: Oh, hadn't he also been at Coral Sea?

van Deurs: No. No, he wasn't at Coral Sea. But his squadron was wiped out at Midway. He was quite a guy.

Q: So he did at least live to achieve what he wanted to do – if he meant it.

van Deurs: I think he meant it. You know, the tough part of it was none of the torpedoes hit.

Q: Ensign Gay was the only one that survived.

van Deurs: Gay survived. He was the only survivor of that strike.

Waldron was quite a man. Aviators like Waldron and myself — most aviators realized that the airplane had quit being a toy; it was a lethal weapon.

But the high command, the black shoe boys, still didn't believe it. It had been kind of a gradual process. You couldn't blame them. These things had gradually improved over twenty years. They'd started out being quite ineffectual, but improvements in planes, engines, weapons, techniques, and skills – they all improved over that period, so that by the time 1940 came along they were pretty dangerous things.

I think probably the White House and most of the high command didn't realize. They didn't realize how deadly planes could be.

Q: And yet they spent the money for carriers ...

van Deurs: Rather grudgingly, rather grudgingly. We had to fight every inch for it.

Q: Did you hate to leave the squadron?

van Deurs: I hated to, very much. It was kind of funny in a way. I asked for a third year, and it was inferred that I'd have it.

In June they moved the squadron from Ford Island over to Kaneohe About the first of August Slim Johnson showed up with orders to relie me. He'd just come out from the Bureau. He said, "I also have a message from Jack Towers for you. He said, 'You won't like it, but you're going to Corpus Christi as the A and R officer. The shops are in trouble down there and they want somebody to run them. You're not going to like it, but you've got to go.'"

I had about two or three months over my two years, then left the squadron with Slim.

I got down to Corpus. The man that was the A and R officer was senior to me, but by that time I'd been selected for Commander and he had not, and he was a bird I detested personally. Most people did. They called him "Herman the VErmin."

The reason the shops were in trouble was, a lot of crooked work. They had two or three thousand employees, but they had never completed an airplane overhaul.

Q: Crooked work?

van Deurs: Crooked work - the shops were building furniture for him, things to be presented to the Commandant ...

Q: Steel ash trays, book ends ...

van Deurs: Yes, all kinds of things.

So I got to Corpus a couple of days early, looked for a place to live, went out to the Air Station to see if I had any mail, checked the exec - he was an old friend, Ross Lyons. Ross said, "Let's see, they have you slated to go over as Assistant to Herman the Vermin, but Harold Fick down in the training department wants you as his Assistant. What do you want to do?" "I'd rather go to the training department." "Let's get Harold."

Harold was one class ahead of me. We talked it over and Harold said, "When so and so was down here from the Bureau they said Van was to go to A and R." "Did the skipper hear him say that?" Ross asked. Harold scratched his head, "No, I don't think so. No, the skipper didn't know about it." "All right, you can go to training."

Herman didn't want me in the shops because as soon as I made my number I'd be senior to him, and he didn't want anybody that could check up on him anyway. It looked like a mess; I didn't want any part of it.

So I was Assistant for training. It was very interesting. The Station was just getting going. The first class was part way through training. The Commandant was Alva Bernhard, who had been my student at primary training years before. I'd never seen him since. I'd kept out of his way. I was surprised, he greeted me like a long lost brother, and I never had anybody more glad to see me in my life.

My boss, Fick, didn't get along with him too well, and it got embarassing, because Fick would go down there and argue for something we needed and get thrown out. I'd say, "Let me try," and go down and put in the same arguments and get it on a silver platter. After a couple of times doing that I quit that because it was just embarrassing Harold, but the Old Man was fine to me.

Corpus Christi was still being built though the Station had been operating for about six months under Commandant Bernhard. The contractor had nothing to do with the Commandant. He worked for the officer-in-charge of Construction, Commander Lou Moeller, CEC, USN, who reported only to the Bureau of Yards and Docks in Washington. Periodically things turned up that were good engineering, but impossible for flying. When we objected Moeller's officers said they had asked an aviator about it and he said it was okay. Usually they could not remember which aviator they asked. After I said that if I wanted a bridge I wouldn't ask the first man that had a CE diploma, I'd look for one experienced in bridges, I found myself with an additional job I became the only aviator to be consulted by the Constructors, and had to pass on all their plans from an aviation point of view.

Moeller named one of his officers as the only one authorized to consult aviation, meaning me. On that basis several of the outlying facilities were designed and completed without further arguments. I found that part of my work very interesting for we had to combine economy of location and construction with the demands for air space and other operating requirements.

Shortly before Pearl Harbor my boss Harold went to England as an observer - a month's job - or boondoggle to see what they were doing.

The curriculum called for the students to drop some live bombs before they finished their training, but we had no targets suitable for them. Harold had been arguing about it for months, and gotten nowhere. We'd leased a lot of training fields down on the King Ranch, but they wouldn't lease us a bombing target. They said that they'd done that during the first war and when the first bomb dropped all of their Mexican cowboys took off for Mexico and their cattle damn near starved before they could get any people back to work. It was bad enough having airplanes, but they wouldn't talk bombing. We had suggested buying Padre Island or buying some land there. The Navy Department said Padre Island was the subject of a trial in the courts between the State of Texas and forty-eight claimants to see who owned it. It was supposed to have oil under it and known to have buried treasure on it, and the Navy was not about to become claimant forty-nine.

While Harold was away this thing got critical. We had students who were finished except for the bombing. My consultant on Moeller's team was Moeller's land agent. He came up with an idea. He said,

"We can make a lease and send it in to the Department for approval, but we can start working as soon as we have it signed here. The only one of those forty-eight who really is in possession is Mr. King, president of one bank uptown. He has a house there he uses for week-ends, runs a few cattle on the island, and he'd be glad to lease us sites for two or three targets at a dollar a year, and if we send it to the Navy Department it might beef up his claim."

So I took that to the boss. He said okay. In a matter of hours the contractor had fenced in the targets to keep the cattle away and we had the kids bombing. I don't think King ever got his dollar a year. The papers went across my desk after the war in the Pentagon, still gathering endorsements, what to do about it, but in the meantime the war's bomber pilots were trained.

About that time we were running a dawn to dark schedule with the Catalinas, dividing students between early and late flying sections. When I dorve onto the Station about 0800 I passed a long line of the seaplane hangers on my way to the Administration Building. Usually the big planes were in the air.

Then one sunny morning with the temperature about eighty degrees plus I saw the planes all on the aprons with not a propeller turning. I hit the office yelling for Dutch Duerfelt, the Operations Officer, and demanded why no planes were in the air. He said a Northerner was due at 0834 with freezing weather and high winds. Doc Lyons, the weather guesser, had been tracking it all night.

I looked out a window across a bay like glass in the sunshine, and said, "Nuts," and sent for Doc.

"Dutch is wrong," the weatherman said, "it will be here at 0832. It's now freezing in Austin. I've been checking it since it was up in Nebraska."

I was still skeptical as the three of us stood by the window, even when a dark cloud appeared beyond the far shore. I stared across twelve miles of placid water and saw a thin white cloud form under the cloud and move quickly toward us. At 0832 a fifty knot blast of cold wind whipped surf against the seawall and launching ramps, sent sand and loose debris flying inland across the station. The temperature dropped twenty degrees in moments.

That afternoon I nearly froze driving to town in nothing but a kahki shirt, the thermometer stood around 20 F. I trusted Doc Lyon's forecasts after that.

Fick came back to Corpus. He had stopped at Washington and heard a rumor that we already knew, that they were going to combine Corpus Christi and Pensacola under an admiral as the Intermediate Training Command with headquarters at Pensacola. Harold had the idea that the way to get to be a captain quick was to be Chief of Staff of that command. He was pretty bitter because some of his classmates had already been spotted to captain and he hadn't. Some of them were junior to him, so he began working all kinds of angles to get to be Chief of Staff at Pensacola.

Admiral Bernhard went to sea, and Admiral E. E. Montgomery took over at Corpus. Monty let Harold go. That was fine. I think the two of them had been together at Norfolk in a squadron about the time I was going to a cruiser. Harold thought he was being very clever secretly politicking all around - it showed like he was doing it on Broadway. He went to Pensacola as Chief of Staff of the big show, and I stayed at Corpus as Superintendent of Aviation Training.

Around this time I discovered that Admiral Montgomery was the fastest reader I ever met. On occasions I handed him an urgent letter, maybe a full page single spaced. He would glance at it, say - that's what I want, sign it, and hand it back to me. At first I thought he was taking a lot on trust, but after it happened several times I found that he knew exactly what he had signed.

Then they organized the Training Center. Our outlying fields had complicated things from the beginning, because the admiral at Corpus was commanding officer of all of them. He was the only one who could hold mast, and if anybody would get in trouble at a field thirty miles away somebody had to bring the accused and witnesses over to bring a man to mast. It was ridiculous. I don't know how many thousand fitness reports went across the admiral's desk every quarter. He couldn't possibly know them all.

For over a year we'd been arguing to make these fields separate commands, with commanding officers who could take care of the discipline problems and so on. The Bureau finally decided to do it, or the Navy Department, and make Corpus a Training Center with a flock of satellite commands - whereupon Monty made me Chief of Staff of the Center as well as holding the training job of the Center. Well, the change meant a new regulation book, for all the administration organization had to change. The question was how do you do it while operating full speed.

I said, "If you let me sit down in the back room without a telephone for about two weeks, I'll write the damned thing."

Well, Monty wouldn't agree. He wanted to start working with the new organization right now, do it with memorandums. Yes, I agreed we could.

So we took a smart j.g. and put him in the back room, told him to start to write a regulation book, while I ran the place by memorandum. Every time I decided something by memorandum I'd send it to the kid who was writing the book. It became part of the book. My telephone got pretty hot. I guess maybe it was two weeks before I had time to go down the long corridor to the Admiral's office. I was using a recorder or jeep like I'd seen at Draim's place, at Norfolk, to take dictation and conversations, and driving my Indian secretary crazy with the stuff I poured into it. They were calling me from all over, "What do we do about this?" "Well, do it this way. I'll cover you with a memorandum"

That went on for a couple of weeks, I guess, before I saw Monty. I was sending the copies of all these things to him. Never heard a word from him. Nobody said boo, as I started taking all the whole place apart. When I saw him I said, "I've been taking your darned Air Station apart and throwing the pieces all around." He said, "You're doing fine, all right with me, keep on going."

So I went back and kept on. That went on for months around there. I left before the regulation book was ever written, I guess, but the thing was running pretty smooth, putting out three hundred a week - pilots.

Q: How large was the station eventually?

van Deurs: Oh gee, I don't know. That was about the peak — when we were graduating three hundred a week.

Q: How long was the training course?

van Deurs: They took their primary training at other stations, and came to us having done primary work. We gave them the basic and the advanced. I don't remember, but the figure comes to mind that we had a cadet load of about five thousand on board and we were putting out three hundred a week, and feeding them in at the same rate. It was a lot of fun.

Q: How long did you say it was, the training course?

van Deurs: I don't remember exactly how long it was, but you could figure it out from that.

Q: Weeks or months?

van Deurs: Oh, it was probably about three or four months.

Q: I read some place that at the top there were about eighteen thousand men, personnel.

van Deurs: There probably were. I don't know, we had over fifteen thousand planes flying all the time.

We put up these satellite stations, some of them as much as fifty miles away, and each one of those had a flock of practice fields around them. While I was still the Assistant they were building the first of those things, and some of the things they built were kind of awkward. As I said the station was not completed when the war started. The officer in charge of construction, and the contractor were still finishing. So as we needed more facilities we just added that onto the contract and kept it going.

Q: Actually Corpus Christi wasn't finished when you went there?

van Deurs: Oh no. They were operating. They'd taken in the first group of students, but they were still building on it.

Q: So you saw it grow from practically nothing up to eighteen thousand people?

van Deurs: Yes, and it was a lot of fun. I always did enjoy building things.

With some fifteen thousand planes operating we had quite a number of crashes, but remarkably few funerals. There was no end to the novel way youngsters could wreck airplanes. Dutch Duerfelt's operation office was in constant touch with flying on all of our stations. Periodically he would pop into my office saying,

"Now I've seen everything. Listen to what just happened ..." Usually he was back in an hour or so contritely saying, "Boss I'll never say again 'I've seen everything,' but maybe I have this time, listen to this one ..."

I only remember a few now, but Corpus logs for that period would make an interesting book for some researcher. For instance –

An instructor fell out of a primary trainer at the top of a loop, leaving a green student aboard to make his first solo landing. Dutch was relieved when the student got down without breaking his neck. But shortly thereafter he was back to say a test pilot had fallen out the same way and the plane was bouncing around the sky with an inexperienced mechanic hanging onto the controls. The men who fell out parachuted safely and we suspected they had forgotten to fasten their safety belts but both denied that. The mech made several attemps to land, but climbed away after each approach. Maybe an hour later he cut the switch a hundred feet in the air and made a perfectly good landing in the middle of a field. Why did he cut the switch? So he couldn't change his mind again, he said.

We found the NAF had put safety blets in backwards in a lot of those planes. If a pilot pulled the stick back to his belly in a loop, his cuff would trip the belt when he moved the stick forward again.

We were busy those days, but life was seldom dull.

Q: How many hours a day were you working at that point?

van Deurs: About fourteen, it got worse later.

Q: Were there any WAVES there while you were there?

van Deurs: Yeah, that was kind of funny. Bernard was still skipper and Harold Fick was still there when we got word that the first WAVE officer was coming down there. SHe'd be followed pretty quick by some WAVE communicators who would take over part of the communication duties. We had rather a complicated radio setup there to keep track of all these planes and the outlying stations were linked there with the operations office. Harold and the Old Man thought this was just horrible. The Navy was shot to hell, bringing the women in - this was terrible.

Q: They hadn't asked for any WAVES?

van Deurs: No, they hadn't asked for any. They had protested. They didn't want them. They thought that was the last word. This was awful.

Personally I couldn't see why it wasn't a good idea. I'd known a lot of smart women. I got thinking about it - both of them were henpecked as hell. Their wives were unattractive and kind of dumb, to my way of thinking. I finally decided that was why they were against WAVES.

They'd have to have special provisions here, they were going to put barbed wire fences around the WAVES quarters with sentries on the gate and run it like a girls boarding school, and so on.

Well, fortunately the first WAVE who showed up was a little bit of a kind of heavyweight ensign who was a physical education major, and some of the young fellows tried to get smart over in the club swimming pool, and she could handle any two of them at once. It was really an education. It was an education to see her make Christians out of these smart guys.

Before the second batch arrived I think Montgomery took over and they were starting the Center. Oh hell, Harold had this thing rigged up - they were allowed liberty till eight o'clock in the evening or some damn thing - oh, Christ, it sounded like a girls' prep school. It was awful.

We got the first batch, radio operators, put them in this air communication room to try them out. They did a better job than the men they replaced. They were doing fine.

By that time it was a Training Center and there was a separate commanding officer of the main station. He put out an order that was very much like one Harold had planned - all kinds of restrictions on these women. I got a copy of the thing, looked at it, hotfooted it down the corridor to the Admiral's office and found him looking at the same damn thing. "Are you thinking what I'm thinking?" He said, "Yeah, if they're taking a man's place, they rate a man's privileges. There may be some sex going on around here, but so what They came in the Navy, they're in the Navy."

Q: Sex is here to stay anyway.

van Deurs: He sent for the station skipper. When Captain George Owen appeared Monty exploded. He got red, then purple, balling George out and explaining that if women were taking men's work, they rated men's privileges. He seemed in a towering rage when he ordered George to get back to his office and cancel the order within five minutes. The minute the door closed he grinned at me and said quietly, "Well, somebody has to be the head man around here."

He was a very swell boss to work for. The order was cancelled and the WAVES were treated like everyone else of the same rate or rank.

Pensacola, probably under Harold's influence, didn't have much luck. I went over for a conference a couple of times, had a few drinks in the club or somewhere with some of their WAVE officers, and they were a pretty unhappy bunch. They had all kinds of strings tied on them over there.

But we ended up with a lot of them as mechanics, and all over the station, and as far as I know they all did a very good job. Monty's theory and mine was that if they wanted to be "nice" girls they still could, if they wanted to be tramps on the outside they could be tramps on the outside, just so they did their job. That's what we got them for - to do a job, not to teach morals or run a school.

Q: I know that there were lots of them eventually at the top peak, there were a large number of them in Corpus.

van Deurs: Oh yes. Oh, we had a hell of a lot of them before I left there, and as far as I know they all did an excellent job. Never made trouble as far as the work goes at all.

Q: Overall I think that was the conclusion in the Navy.

van Deurs: I was very happy with them.

Q: Did you ever have any working for you personally?

van Deurs: The communication setup was under my thumb.

Q: Were you through with that?

Oh, I wanted to ask you where you were on Pearl Harbor Day.

van Deurs: I was in Corpus Christi.

Q: Do you remember what you did, what your reactions were?

van Deurs: The quarters weren't finished on the Air Station. We were living in town, and according to my peacetime routine in those days I was doing a little sleeping in on Sunday morning, when my daughters turned on the radio and came running in and said, "Hey Daddy, the Japanese are bombing Pearl Harbor just like you said they would."

So I got in the car and went out to the Station and that was the last Sunday that I got to sleep for a long time.

Q: Did the activities increase drastically at Corpus then?

van Deurs: Oh, tremendously. Radford was the head man in training in Washington at the time, and Radford had seen the thing coming. They'd been periodically boosting the intake of students, and in thenext few months he turned the whole training system upside down in order to accommodate more. When we started we were giving primary training and basic, the whole works, and it was pretty obvious that that wouldn't suffice.

We'd get a phone call from Radford, "Hey, have you got the machine on?" Yeah, put on the recorder. For about fifteen minutes he'd explain how they were changing things and what he wanted us to do to live up to it and so on, and I'd take the record off the recorder and throw it to the boys in the back room and say, "Listen to this and get going."

The system changed. It finally worked out so that we sent all our primary training planes to what had been reserve air stations and some new ones that they commandeered, commerical fields or something, and started using as stations, and used them for primary training. A lot of this was under separate command in Kansas City. Cadets leaving these bases had to have so much, be able to do certain things, and then they were sent to Corpus or Pensacola for the basic.

We began getting people from places like Spokane and San Diego and various odd joints that didn't have the training they were supposed to have completed. We no longer had the planes to give it. So it was pretty much of a problem to start in with.

The only way we were allowed to communicate with the primary training stations was through Washington and Kansas City, the chain of command. That was obviously too slow, so I flew up to Kansas City. The Chief of Primary Training there was, I guess, Buckmaster. I think Buckmaster may have been; I'm not sure about that. He did inherit that after the Battle of Midway. But the Chief of Staff was Indian Joe Tomlinson, who had been an early naval aviator and had resigned in the twenties to go to TWA, which was Trans-Continental Western Air in those days, and did most of the pioneer work on instrument flying for the airlines. He developed the system to let the airlines fly at night, and so on. He kept his commission in the Reserves, and he'd been called up.

Indian Joe was a couple of classes senior to me and he was quite a go-getter, so we just made an unofficial deal. When something went wrong, we got some of these people that hadn't had the proper training, I'd send Indian Joe a personal message. He got in an airplane and flew out to the station that was doing it wrong and set 'em right. We never had any more trouble with that one. That worked beautifully for several months there. A purely unofficial deal, but it cured that sort of trouble.

In the meantime these changes kept coming, and Radford would call up, "What do you need to take so many more cadets?"

That meant so many planes, so many planes meant so many mechanics, to house the students and the mechanics you needed so many barracks. To feed them you needed so much mess hall space, and so on. So it was kind of a complicated problem.

Some of my smart boys finally built a big diagram. It had barracks and mess halls and all the things that went into this, including fields and whathaveyou, against the training load, so that I could take those kind of messages from Radford, hand the recording to these kids, and inside of an hour they were already back saying, "It will take so many barracks, so many this and that, and cost so many million."

We usually got the go-ahead, and the contractors' people were told to start building. It worked pretty well.

Q: That was the only advantage, if you can think of war having any advantage, that you did go ahead and do what you had to do without getting ...

van Deurs: Radford would usually take the rap for the money, say, "You go ahead and start doing it. I'll see that it's cleared up here."

Pensacola didn't have that good a setup. They never did get wise. They got stumped on these things a couple of times and said, "Oh, we don't need anything," and then when the people showed up they had a hell of a time.

The pay-off came — Radford called up with one of those problems, and I've forgotten - we figured something twenty million and a new field, barracks, mess hall, and so on, and Pensacola said they didn't need anything. Radford called up the next day and told me to go over to Pensacola and have a conference and see if we couldn't get together on this, see why the figures were so different. So I grabbed an airplane and my number one helper ...

Q: Did you fly it?

van Deurs: Yes. There was a SeaBee wanted to go for the ride so I put him in the back end. It was a little two engine five passenger Beachcraft. The weather was kind of bad. We told them, give us contact flight clearance, and taxied out to the end of the runway after lunch, soon as I got through with the telephone call as a matter of fact. Then the tower called us, said the airways wouldn't give a release for visual flight rules. So I said, "Well, clearance for five hundred feet on top." We got that and we took off and climbed through some little stuff and flew along five hundred feet on top, a lot more wind than we expected, getting late. Finally we were up at twelve thousand feet with our wheels dragging on the top of clouds, and it had been solid under us for a couple of hours. I knew we were over the beacon at New Orleans. The sun was just going down in this stuff so I said - we'd better stop at New Orleans. We called New Orleans tower and asked them, and they had a silly code. I don't know why the weather on American airwaves had to be confidential in those days - what good it could do the enemy - but it had to be. Every day had a sheet, a code, with lette that meant different kinds of weather.

Q: Different kinds of weather conditions?

van Deurs: Yes.

This bird in the tower gave us XYZ or whatever it was. We looked on the sheet and it said, "Clear and unlimited." We got a repeat. It turned out later they'd given us yesterday's sheet. Finally he broke down and said, "The ceiling is five hundred feet and it's raining like hell."

I turned around to Van Every in the other seat and said, "Hey, Van, do you know an instrument card? Are you qualified as an instrument pilot?" He said, "No, Boss, I haven't got one that's current. Have you?" "No, I haven't got one, mine expired a long time ago." "How are we going to get down? It ain't legal for us to get down in this without an instrument card." The poor SeaBee in the back seat was about ready to jump out.

So we went down illegally and made it all right.

Q: How could you get down through the clouds?

van Deurs: They had a system then - probably do about the same thing now. They told us to come down to four thousand feet and hold on a certain beam from the airport beacon. The beacon sent out beams in four directions, and to hold on the west beam at four thousand feet. There was somebody else landing down below. Then they'd tell us to come on and drop down. We had a pattern of going around this field.

Q: So they did talk you in.

van Derus: Oh yes. Well, they'd tell you when to come in. They didn't have the GCA or anything like that at the time, but you had a pattern that you flew on this beacon, so you knew about where you were in relation to the airport. And as soon as you got down below five hundred feet you could see through the rain to some extent.

Q: Boy, you were awful low then.

van Deurs: We spent the night there, and were socked in the next morning. Then we got a phone call there saying to come back to Corpus, that people from Washington and Pensacola were all coming over there for a conference. So we got out of there.

The Admiral and Fick with some more people came over from Pensacola. Radford and the Assistant Secretary for Air and his Aide and a couple of civilian experts came down from Washington, and sat around this table. The Aide was a classmate of mine, Joe Bolger, that liked long cigars.

We said, "Before we start this conference we got this All Nav message last night that said any materials that were going to be delivered in the next six months, the orders had to be on the manufacturer's factory books by midnight tonight - some kinds of material it calls for, steel, pipe, all kinds. We're going to have to make this change and we need a lot of materials and they've got to be ordered before midnight, not the requisition written, but actually on the manufacturer's books."

Q: What time of day was this?

van Deurs: This was ten o'clock in the morning. So, can we go ahead and start ordering? There was a new officer in charge of construction that loved to do things in a hurry, an old white-haired man, and if you told him to build something that was all right. If you told him to build it before tomorrow - oh that's what he liked, he'd really get going.

Q: You were lucky then.

vanDeurs: Oh, yes, he was swell. Can't think of his name now - he was an old Reserve that had been pulled in, had been a civil engineer all his life, and he was all primed. He had the lists he'd need of materials for this field, and he had a flock of people standing by telephones ready to start ordering the minute we got a "go" on it.

The Secretary looked at this All Nav and said he'd never seen it, didn't know anything about that. "There's a telephone here? I'll call my office in Washington," and he started trying to get Washington. I watched Joe Bolger, his Aide, with this black cigar, staring at the ceiling, blowing smoke rings, a big grin on his face. Finally Gates got through to his office, and they didn't know anything about that order, they hadn't heard of it - call Ben Moreell who was head of Bureau of Yards and Docks. Finally Gates was getting madder and madder, having troubles with operators, but finally he got through to Moreell's office, and they wouldn't believe it was the Assistant Secretary calling from Texas, and wouldn't put him through to Moreell.

They wouldn't believe him. By this time this guy was getting purple, and Joe's grin was way up in his hair, and the smoke rings were going to beat the band. Gates never did get any satisfaction out of them.

Q: Did they ever put him through?

van Deurs: No, he never did get any satisfaction out of Washington at all. He tried two or three other things and nobody had an answer So we started in with this huddle.

Q: That should have given him a good idea of the problems in the field, I should think.

van Deurs: Well, at the lunch break I got hold of Joe and said, "Why the hell were you grinning so when your boss was on that telephone?" He said, "Well, you know in Washington he's got a couple of secretaries and two or three Marines that spend their lives getting through on telephones for him, and he gives them all hell, because when he wants to talk to somebody and they haven't gotten them instantly, and I just loved seeing him trying to do it himself and getting crossed up."

We started in with this huddle and said, "In order to do this, what do you need?" "We can work so many airplanes around a field and keep them going and then we run out of air space, so we need a new field over here, that'll cost so much."

"Pensacola, what are you doing about it?" "Well, we haven't thought about that." "Maybe you ought to have another field too."

"Well, now if we put in a field we'll need so many barracks for the mechanics, so many barracks for the cadets, this that and the other thing, and that costs so much."

We brought in our funny board that had it all tabulated, "That will cost so much."

"What have you done about that, Pensacola?" "We haven't done anything about that." "Well, you'd better put that on your list."

Everything that came up, after the Secretary argued about it and got convinced with our figures, each time he'd turn around and tell Pensacola to do it.

Q: Didn't they begin feeling silly?

van Deurs: I don't know.

Finally, I guess about one o'clock or so he said, "Well, I don't know. We've got to have these things and we've got to do it, and I haven't any authority to spend this money, but I'll fight with Secretary Knox when I get back about it. You go ahead and order the material."

I passed the word to my SeaBee friend out the door, he took off on a dead run. About five o'clock in the afternoon he called me and said, "Everything is ordered. It's coming from all over."

That was how Beaville got built, which they're still using.

Q: That was a terribly demanding job, but I would think of some satisfaction to you.

van Deurs: It was a lot of fun, building. And that conference was a lot of fun, because all these people came down there prepared to hang us on the top of a Christmas tree or something, and ended up taking our figures on the whole business.

Q: You were obviously prepared for it. That makes the difference.

van Deurs: I was kind of glad that I left Corpus before they began cutting down. Shortly after I left they realized that pilots were coming out now faster than they would need them to make up losses. At first we were qualifying a lot of them for the new carriers that were being built. In the summer of '43 they caught up with that and then they began slowing down in the training program a little bit, and the fun was gone, but I'd left by that time.

Q: Did you hate being away from the Pacific? I'm sure you didn't because you recognized you were making it possible for the Pacific War to be fought.

van Deurs: Well, I didn't like being ashore when something was going on, and I had a lot of friends out there. I had a lot of friends killed at Pearl Harbor. I felt like I ought to be out there.

At the same time, knowing what they were building in ships and know ing what we were turning out in pilots and planes, I knew darned well it would be more fun to be there when we were winning instead of retreating, and that the day would come. The tide was bound to turn with the production that was coming along.

Q; Were you aware of Midway?

van Deurs: Only what was in the newspapers, until a classmate walked into my office one morning and said he'd flown in on a NATS about midnight and found a room over at BOQ, and wondered if I could get him over to Laredo. I said - yeah, that was easy, I would get a plane and send him over - why? He said his wife had been down in Mexico and he had thirty days leave and they wouldn't let him into Mexico in wartime in a uniform, so she was going to come out and meet him at Laredo, and they were going on leave.

"Well, where are you drawing your pay when you're not on leave?" He looked around, and we were alone and the door was closed, and he said, "I had a nice destroyer, but I ain't got it no more."

"What happened?" Then he told me that he was the skipper of the one that was alongside the YORKTOWN when she was torpedoed, the HAMMON, and he was blown into the water and pretty badly banged up by the explosives and he'd just gotten out of the hospital and was on survivor leave.

Q: You hadn't known about the YORKTOWN being lost?

van Deurs: We hadn't heard anything about the YORKTOWN being lost.

Before that, after the Battle of Coral Sea, somebody flew in from the West Coast and said, "I don't know what's going on, but something's happened to the LEXINGTON." "How do you know?"

"Well, I was in Long Beach and Jakie Fitch and all his staff came ashore looking for a tailor shop to buy some new clothes. Something's happened."

Q: Admiral Stroup said people kind of had some idea in Long Beach and San Diego because they had told their wives to get them some new clothes.

van Deurs: Things like that trickle through.

There's one interesting thing - right at the start of Corpus, just before the war, in fact I think about two weeks before the war, they were doing a lot of training down there in Catalinas. And my old squadron had dumped their old planes at San Diego and flown back to Pearl Harbor with new ones, and they wanted to fly some of those planes to Corpus for training. And I got permission to take, I think, either three or four crews to San Diego to bring them planes back and had orders to make it a daytime flight because there were no night landing facilities at Corpus yet. My brother-in-law was stationed at San Diego; I put up at their house. The first night there was a big party. I got a couple of hours sleep. We had to take-off about daylight to make it before dark, to Texas. I got a couple of hours sleep and got out to the air station and got these planes warmed up - and the fog rolled in. By eight o'clo it was too late to start, so we cut them off and I went back to the house and got a couple of hours sleep, and then partied again that night, and did it over again. It happened three or four days in a row. Finally - Admiral McCain was head man on North Island at the time, Commander Fleet Air - I went around and told him, "My orders are to make a daylight flight out of this, but the fog's been catching me every morning, and this damn brother-in-law of mine is trying to kill me. If I stay here and keep up with him on the drinking a couple of more nights you can bury me. So let me take-off at night and make a night flight out of it, and we'll have enough gas to circle till daylight if we can't see to land there, but I think we can all right. It's a big bay, we'll get down all right."

The first pilots I'd brought with me I knew were good Catalina pilots. "Okay, sure son, go ahead, God dammit, son" --

I told you he had false teeth and they didn't fit too well, and they kind of clicked. He'd go clickety click, "God dammit son," clickety click.

So we got out of there about five in the afternoon, with the fog just rolling in behind us, and went high enough to make sure that we missed all the mountains, and headed for Texas. I've never been colder in my life. I'd gone west with nothing but a leather jacket and there weren't any heaters in the planes. Somebody'd stolen the percolator so that the galley wasn't working, and they gave us some coffee in thermos bottles. That was ice cold before we got past El Paso. It was so damn cold we kept going to sleep in the seat. It was awful.

The second pilot I had was not an expert and he was not used to night flying, and a couple of times letting him handle the thing, I'd wake up and find him all cocked up on one ear with vertigo from the lights and have to take over. I never had more trouble staying awake in my life, and I've never been colder than I was in that silly airplane that night.

Oh, we made it all right, but it wasn't fun. The only good fun in the thing was - they didn't send flight plan reports on military planes at that time, on account of they began to go in for secrecy before Pearl Harbor.

I called the El Paso tower and said, "Three Navy seaplanes, twelve thousand feet over El Paso, heading so and so." A sleepy voice said, "Hup, what is that? You say seaplanes?"

Q: So you got down safely anyway.

van Deurs: Oh, yeah, we got there and landed, and I went home and slept for a couple of days I think. It was a lot of fun.

Q: That was before the war?

van Deurs: Yes, about two weeks before Pearl Harbor.

Q: And how did you get out of Corpus, then?

van Deurs: Montgomery was fighting to get a carrier command at sea, and he promised me to take me with him. Before that happened my brother-in-law, Fish Moebus, had been over at Jacksonville and was ordered down to the South Pacific as Admiral Fitch's Chief of Staff. I sent him a postcard and said, "You're getting the only job in this war I'd like, how about getting me on the team?"

He got down to the South Pacific and told Fitch I wanted a spot down there. Fitch had been very good to me at Pearl Harbor so he immediately asked the Navy Department to send me down there.

Well, Monty wouldn't turn me loose, and so there was a long series of dispatches back and forth, South Pacific asking for me and the Bureau stalling one way or another.

In April 1943, Monty flew up to Washington for something and came back and said, "They promised me I could have a command at sea in July, and at that time you can go as my Chief of Staff, or you can go with Admiral Fitch. You can have your choice."

This put me in a bad spot. There were two very fine guys offering me jobs, and I didn't want to say no to either of them. But about two days later, the Admiral sent for me and told me to get on the phone Washington was coming through. He used to do that frequently with a call coming in, both of us listen in and we could cross-check on what was said. It was the Bureau of Personnel. They called up to apologize to the Admiral, but they were writing my dispatch orders to the South Pacific. They realized that they were going back on the promise they'd given him two days before, but they had had an urgent message from down there that they needed me right away so they were sending me orders to proceed immediately, gave me twelve hours to get out of Corpus. So that was that.

The children were in school. We were in quarters. They were nice enough to say Ann could stay in quarters till the end of the school term. I threw two bottles of brandy and two khaki shirts into a suitcase, took off, and left Ann with all the problem

Q: Oh dear. How did you get out there?

van Deurs: I'd been working pretty hard. I got somebody to fly me up to Dallas, and jumped on the Southern Pacific. I thought a couple of days in a pullman would be a rest; that was a mistake. It was the slowest, dirtiest, lousiest ride I ever had in a railroad train.

Got to Los Angles, went to get on the LARK and on the platform I ran into an old friend from high school days in Portland, who was working for Kaiser at the time. He was getting on the LARK and he had a bottle of whiskey so we talked old times half the nigh Got to San Francisco and the town was full of people waiting for transportation to the Pacific. Every hotel was full of them.

They took one look at my orders — the orders said I had to be there by a certain date. "Well, we'll get you out of here this afternoon." I said, "Wait a minute, I've got a lot of friends in this town. Make it tomorrow." So they did.

Q: By air?

van Deurs: I went out of here in one of the old Pan-American Clippers, seaplane things, to Pearl. I was senior enough to commandeer one of the bunks in it. They had a certain number of staterooms built in, and I had a very nice sleep. I think we got away about midnight from Treasure Island and I slept soundly until we got to Pearl.

But they chased me on out of there to Epiritu Santo. I landed at a little shack on the beach. "Captain Moebus just called up, he'dll be down here with a jeep to pick you up. He's on his way down now."

I got in the jeep and asked Fish why I had to be there on the 22nd, what's happening? He said, "Oh, nothing. In about a month we're going to capture Munda, but there isn't anything really scheduled till then." I said, "Why in the dickens did my orders say I had to be here on the 22nd?"

"Well," he said, "We got tired of being stalled by the Bureau, so the Admiral and I figured that if we put a date in our request that didn't give them time to argue, would just give them time to get you here without any argument back and forth, it might work. So we picked that date and said we needed you by that time, and they didn't have time to debate, so they sent you."

So that was how I got out of Corpus.

During that month before Munda, Fitch sent me all around the South Pacific to see all the islands that we had anything on, because he wanted me to work as his Plans Officer - give me a look at what we were planning with. So I visited Guadalcanal, our most forward base at the time. I also visited Noumea and Efati, and when they had set up a certain number of fields and bases behind that, in case we didn't hold the Guadalcanal line. I went over to Nandi in the Fijis and Wallace Island and several other places. Somewhere along the line, I suspect it was Guadalcanal, I picked up a swell case of malaria, but that didn't break out till a bit later.

The tour was rather interesting in several ways. On Wallace Island, which was a French island, I got a very very low opinion of the French colonial administration. The natives were nice people and completely looted and downtrodden. There was a little hospital there run by a couple of French nuns, apparently, that was -- all. The natives were horribly in need of medical care, but the governor was uninterested in any of it. He had some Marines there that had built a field and they were doing what they could for some of these people, but the French were paying no attention to them at all. Down in Noumea the same thing. Halsey had had to tell the governor to go back in the corner and sit down, he was taking over. And we had several fields on New Caldonia.

The French used indentured labor. The Tonkinese from what's now Vietnam, would sign on for five years, and go down there and work on a plantation, or work on the nickel mines of New Caledona. Thenthe French trick apparently was to mistreat them so that they'd run away before the five years was out and then they wouldn't have to pay 'em. A lot of these poor people would come out of the jungle and our GIs and Marines that were running the airfields would feed them and put them to work and try to make friends with them. But the French were pretty brutal with all those things.

As far as I know there was only one good Frenchman in the South Pacific, and he was a man named Freddie LeBorge. I suspect that he was the model for Mitchener's Frenchman in his tale of the South Pacific. Freddie had a plantation on Espiritu Santo that was a bit north of the last field we built, one of the fighter strips manned by Marines. He had a wife who lived down in Noumea because the children were in school down there, and so he lived with a Tonkinese mistress on the plantation. He took her everywhere and introduced her, "This is not my wife, it's my mistress," a very cute looking little gal.

But most of the Frenchmen had gone out there to make some money and get back to France, so they lived out of tin cans in a shack and worked the natives for all they were worth to make some dough so they could go back to France.

I always suspected that Freddie couldn't go back to France. Maybe the cops wouldn't let him, or something. But at least he had built a decent house, lived decently, planted vegetables, had something to eat besides canned stuff, kept a cellar of decent wine, and lived rather well.

All the plantations ran cattle through the coconut groves. They'd clear the jungle, plant coconut trees and then plant grass under the trees. To keep the jungle from coming back they'd keep a few cows eating the grass. None of them ever thought of milking a cow or using it for meat except LeBorge. He did both.

He heard that the fighter pilots down on this air strip near him hadn't had any fresh meat for a long time, were eating out of cans, so he butchered a steer and sent it down as a present.

We had him down for dinner one night, sitting next to him, his English was rather broken, I asked him what his plantation was like. I'd heard from some of the people who went up there about the way he lived. "Oh," he said, "It stinks. It stinks." That's all he'd say about it, "It stinks."

Then he kind of grinned and said, "I don't want you fellows coming up there and building another fighter strip."

At Espiritu Santo, the channel between Espitiru Santo and a little island, was a beautiful anchorage. It was the backup point for Guadalcanal. All the stuff that came out of the States was brought in there and then forwarded as we could get it up to the Canal which was about six hundred miles. They'd built a naval base there with a lot of loading piers and docks and cleared big storage areas, and also had a couple of divisions of troops that were staging there most of the time, and we had taken over a lot of plantations to do that.

The camp I was in was on top of a ridge in a coconut grove, a bunch of Dallas huts, to live in, very pleasant and comfortable really, big high powered radio. Fitch was the ComAir. He was also the second senior man in the South Pacific, Halsey's number two. We had an area that had a wire fence around it with about four or five Quonset huts inside, and a gate about twenty feet wide, I gues There was usually a Marine on duty at the gate. Inside there was all the intelligence stuff, the radio, and all the planning. We didn't have a safe, but everything inside that compound was marked "secret."

Nobody worried about it except my Chief Yeoman. I saw him looking at a piece of paper, looking in the desk drawer, in the filing cabinet — "What's the matter?" "Well," he said, "I've got a piece of paper here that's not even marked 'confidential,' and I haven't any place to file it."

Q: Espiritu is where your headquarters were?

van Deurs: Espiritu Santo, yes. It was in the New Hebrides, six hundred miles south of Guadalcanal and about the same distance north of Noumea. That was where we ran the planes and everything else, convoys and what have you, on to Guadalcanal.

Q: How large an establishment was it?

van Deurs: Oh, probably twenty or thirty thousand men on the island. They had a couple of divisions training and what not. We had, I think, two fighter strips. They were building another big bomber strip when I got there. It was quite a big establishment.

It was kind of funny — when the West Coast was blacked out and Honolulu was blacked out, that place burned lights around the clock. We were handling cargo twenty-fours a day down on the waterfront, and two or three times a month when the moon was full the Jap Navy suddenly got one or two seaplanes down there to raid the place. Our radars would signal condition "red," all the lights would go out, and Washing Machine Charlie would come along and throw a couple of bombs into the jungle somewhere and go back again, and as soon as he went off of the radars the lights came on and the loading went on same as before.

Q: What were your offices like?

van Deurs: Oh, a couple of desks in a quonset hut. Maps marked "secret" plastered all over the walls and everything else. That was where we worked.

A couple of things re the chap I relieved, I said, "What have you got planned?" "Well, our really advance planning is how to get enough gasoline to Guadalcanal for tomorrow." It had been pretty tight down there. "Beyond that we haven't got any plans." "Well, what are we trying to do?"

Q: You were Plans Officer?

van Deurs: He was Plans Officer, and I was relieving him.

"What's the object of the war? What are we trying to accomplish?" Well, he didn't know. He guessed maybe to take Rabual some day. But there wasn't any real plan, didn't know. And so ..

Q: How could he be Plans Officer?

van Deurs: It had been a hand to mouth operation. Everybody had been so darned busy just hanging onto the toehold on Guadalcanal that they hadn't had time to think beyond that.

Q: It was just touch and go as to whether they'd hold on.

van Deurs: It had been that close. He was a perfectly good man, but they'd just finally, about the time I got there, got the Japs off Guadalcanal.

Q: That was about May, '43?

van Deurs: Yes. And nobody had thought much beyond that. They were building some fields on the Russell Islands, which the Japs had abandoned too, about twenty miles or so behind Guadalcanal. But beyond that there hadn't been much planning.

Well, then, when I was doing that traveling around, I kept talking to pilots, particularly squadron commanders, who were at Guadalcanal or any place I could find them, about how far they could go with a load of bombs or to pull a fight and get back. Up until the war the Bureau of Aeronautics used to publish a sheet of characteristics of airplanes that showed how fast each plane would go, how far, what it could carry, and so on. Well, those sheets were made up to outshine the Air Corps and impress Congressmen, I guess, because the speeds and the ranges and so on were figured with a completely light airplane under optimum conditions at sea level and so on, and the bomb load and so on was the most we could carry if you left out half the gasoline or something - it didn't match up. When you got in a war those sheets were completely meaningless. I went around and asked everybody how far we could go, what they could do.

Q: You were really doing basic research at that point.

van Deurs: Sort of. I ended up by making myself a little table that gave me a bit of leeway, but for combat operations - why this type would go so far and so on. And they were the figures that the pilots that were flying that particular type had given me.

I put it under the glass on my desk and began using that as one of my tools. Various people came in and said, "Where did you get that? I've been wanting that for a long time. I want that dope." I said, "I made it." "Well, give me a copy."

So some obliging guy there photostatted a flock of them. They got scattered around the South Pacific.

Some time a couple of months later - (I used to go to Guadalcanal periodically with the boss for a few days) I went up there when some enemy ships had been damaged in a night fight, and at daylight they were trying to get some planes up there to finish them off. Mitscher, the Air Commander on Guadalcanal at the time, broke out a copy of my chart -- "Well, this won't go, this won't go." Some Army planes, the longest legged things they had, would just miss it by about ten miles. I begged him to send it anyway, said, "I made that chart and there's ten miles leeway."

"No, sir, that's what the chart says and that's the limit." He wouldn't listen to me. Nobody sent 'em.

So I cursed myself for ever giving anybody a copy of my own calculations. But he stuck to it, no sir, he wasn't going to send a plane an inch beyond what this chart said. I don't think he ever believed that I made the chart, but I did.

After talking to various people on Halsey's staff — it turned out the object was to neutralize, or take, Rabaul. The only way we could advance up the islands was with air cover. They'd already set up the assault on Munda when I got there. I got in on some of the air planning for it.

The Japanese could bring down a terrific amount of air from Bougainville to the place we intended to land. We couldn't reach Bougainville with anything we had to attack them on the ground. And the most we could figure on keeping a patrol over the landing force was about three planes, the distance they had to take-off from Guadalcanal, and go up there and mill around, and come back.

Q: Bougainville or Munda?

van Deurs: Munda. We could keep three fighters over Munda, which was nothing at all if the Japs came in force.

Oh, the week before Munda people went all over the South Pacific looking for airplanes. We were trying to figure out how we could get some more airplanes.

The Army brigadier said, "I was over at Nandi and I saw a couple of fighters on the field over at Nandi. "I don't know whether they'll fly or not, couple of P-51s." So he sent two pilots to Nandi. "If they'll fly, take 'em to Guadalcanal."

Somebody else said, "I heard there was a ship at Noumea that had some planes in crates. Send somebody down there. Knock the crates off, if they'll fly take them to Guadalcanal."

Just scraping everything we could get, and it still figured out at about three airplanes on patrol. Before it came off I went to Halsey, showed him the figures, and begged him to ask for just one more fighter squadron.

I learned later that King had told him that there was nothing more for the South Pacific, there wasn't anything more he could have, and not to ask for anything, do the best he could with what he had, period.

Halsey wasn't about to ask for anything. He looked over my figures. He looked at what the Japs could throw at us. We had photographs of their fields. We had planes that could get that far and take a photograph, but not planes that could get that far and do a bombing job. He said, "Yeah, they could come to us that way, but I've got a hunch they're not going to, so we're going ahead anyway." And he was right.

People called him slapdash and so on, but really it was a purely calculated risk. He knew what we had, and we got away with it. They came down, but they came down by driblets, and we managed to break even on it. They did some damage.

Q: Had the Japs built the airfield on Munda at the time you were there?

van Deurs: Yes, but we'd shot it up with cruisers and bombed it, so that they weren't using it. It was pretty well wrecked.

3 van Deurs - 412

Q: I read it some place that they built it by camouflage by holding nets on top of the trees so that you couldn't see it, so that it wasn't possible to see the work being done on the ground.

van Deurs: I don't know. If they tried that it wasn't very effective, because cruisers went up there and bombarded the place, and bombed it. We could reach it with the bombers from Guadalcanal all right. We pockmarked the thing so that they couldn't use it.

Q: On the other hand, didn't they have a lot of people with ability to repair awfully fast?

van Deurs: They didn't repair that fast. We really plastered that before the assault.

There was one interesing phase of the thing - when I joined the staff they told me I had a civil engineer that was supposed to be working for me in the organization, that he was up there on New Georgia in the jungle. Bill Painter was a Reserve SeaBee, Lieutenant Commander, I think, and one of the most unusual characters I ever ran into. If you listened to him he'd built everyting in China. He'd built drydocks, he'd built skyscrapers, he'd built Shanghai, he'd built everything. Pretty nearly everybody put him down as a boasting blowhard. The other SeaBees wouldn't have him; that was why he ended up on Fitch's staff. He was one of these guys who had to run the show or he wouldn't play. According to Bill he could do anything.

Well, they sent him — landed him from a PT boat, submarine, or something, on the south end of Georgia with a couple of other people and they spent two or three weeks dodging the Japs crawling through the jungle in New Georgia. We wanted to get a fighter field in quick to support that Munda operation, and the missionaries who had been up there had given us a couple of locations where they thought a field could be built. We sent Painter to check; we weren't too sure the missionaries knew what it took to build an airfield.

At the south end of New Georgia was the Segi plantation. It have been famous before the war. A man who'd lived there as a planter for years was a famous host in the South Pacific. There was a big lagoon. It was famous for its sports fishing. Big name people like Jack London and so on had visited there and tried the fishing, every famous sports man you ever heard of. It was the South end; at the north end of this island was Munda.

Painter found Kennedy, the coast watcher, living in the Segi plantation house, an Australian coast watcher with a radio and a bunch of natives. This bird Kennedy was one of the — well, all the coast watchers were unusual characters, but he was one of the wildest. And he'd gone on the theory that if the Japs never saw him they wouldn't know where he was, so every Jap that ever saw him died. In doing it, he'd armed a flock of natives with Japanese equipment. He had a little private army there, and was watching all the trails down to Segi.

Bill Painter went back to the Segi plantation when he got through with his mission and we picked him up there.

The first time I met Bill was when he came into camp after the experience and typed up about a three page report of his travels. He sat in a hut that night and read it to Moebus and me. It said the locations the missionaries had picked out were impossible - one was a swamp and another one was something else, and it would take months to build airfields there. He'd looked at several other things and they were no good. But down at the Segi plantation, it was possible to knock down some coconut trees and put in a four thousand foot fighter strip with water at each end on a peninsula. He thought it could be done in thirty days, from the time the bulldozers were landed from an LST.

Moebus questioned the thirty days. Bill said, "Oh hell, anybody could do it in fifteen, any damn fool could do it in fifteen. I put in thirty to be sure. If a guy's really good he could get a field there in ten days. There are no Japs there right now. If we sent in a survey party ahead of time they could stake out the grade, the bulldozers could come off the LSTs and just start knocking trees down along the row of stakes. Do it in ten days easy, if a guy's good, but any damn fool could do it in fifteen."

Moebus said, "You are sitting at the desk. We'll have to change that last paragraph a little bit. I'll dictate, you write. First go back and change that thirty to fifteen. Put this on for a last paragraph: 'It's recommended that Commander William Painter, the civil engineer on my staff, be made the officer-in-charge-of-construction, and that he be landed ten days ahead of time with a survey party of his own choosing to lay out the field."

While he wrote Bill kept shouting, "You're cutting my throat, you sons-of-bitches, you're cutting my throat!"

Moebus said, "Now, we won't say anything to Admiral Halsey about this, but if you don't get that field done in ten days, we'll spread it all over the South Pacific - what you said about any damn fool could do it in fifteen."

That was what happened, except that the night before Painter and the survey party were supposed to land, we got a radio from the coast watcher, Kennedy, saying that a couple of companies of Japs were landing in the Segi plantation. He was taking to the jungle, and he suggested - since we had some Marines about ready for the Munda assault that the next day we land some Marines on the waterfront and he would have his jungle boys at the end of the jungl and between them they'd get the Japs. That's what was done. We sent some landing craft up there in a hurry with, I don't know, maybe a battalion of Marines. The Japs headed for the jungle and at the edge of the jungle were all these natives that Kennedy had armed with Japanese rifles, and none of the Japs got away.

The next day we sent Bill Painter up, and ...

Q: Is that a story that's well known? I had not read of that.

van Deurs: I've published it in the <u>Naval Institute</u> PROCEEDINGS (October 1958) as "The Segi Man."

Anyway Painter got the field going in ten days. He ran into some unexpected trouble. The first coral he got was no good, had to find some more, and I don't think he took his shoes off in those ten days. He lost twenty pounds. When I got in there after the field was declared open, he looked like a living skeleton. Most of the SeaBees looked the same way, but we were landing fighters there within ten days after the bulldozers went in.

Q: Incredible, isn't it.

van Deurs: It was quite a job. After that, we let the guy boast. We let Bill shoot off his face after that. He did a pretty good job.

We sent him into the jungle two or three other times, up the line, and asked Bill to okay the location of every field we ever built after that, except at Bougainville. We didn't have any good way to get him in, so he did that job from the back end of a Catalina, just over the treetops. Looking over the location we'd picked on the charts, and finally came back and said he thought it could be done.

Q: After Guadalcanal was fairly safe, how did you make your plans then? How did you operate?

van Deurs: What I did - after that scare about the fighters over Munda, I figured how far from one of our fields we could give effective cover to a landing with the planes we had. Then I drew a flock of circles on a chart of the Solomons. From Munda I picked out an island near the edge of that circle and said, "Well, we'll put the next field here," and drew a circle around that. In that way it took us all the way to Empress Augusta Bay on Bougainville, from there we could put everything onto Rabaul.

I don't know, I probably had a bad time - it took me some time to work this thing out - what the plans would do and so on. In the meantime Fitch was yelling for plans, and I think Moebus defended my nose and kept him off my back long enough for me to finish the job.

Q; The planes were going from field to field? What were the planes on the aircraft carriers doing?

van Deurs: We didn't have any carriers then.

Q: Wasn't the SARATOGA there then?

van Deurs: The SARATOGA was there part of the time, and towards the tail end of the campaign some of the others came down there, but they'd lost too many carriers in between the islands there. It was too confined really for the big carriers, the fast carriers.

Q: To operate effectively.

Van Deurs: All that South Pacific campaign was done with land-based air, which was under Fitch. It consisted of: the 13th Air Force; a couple of Marine Air Wings; four or five Navy squadrons of various types, fighters, long-range patrol land planes and Catalina and the New Zealand Air Force. They were all working together.

It was the only really unified outfit that I saw during the war, because day after day it happened that there wasn't enough. Nobody had enough airplanes, enough pilots to put on a raid.

So they'd get together the night before, at the headquarters that Mitscher had when I first went down there - they called it ComAir Solomons. He had a staff that was organized with a fighter command, a bomber command, and something else. Anyway those were the three operators, and it was a mixed staff - it was Army, Navy, Marines, everybody was on it. And they'd get together - "All right, we have to send a raid on the line tomorrow. How many fighters?"

Well, the New Zealanders had enough fighters to fly high cover, and somebody else had a bunch of torpedo planes that could lug the bombs, and maybe the Army had some planes that could fly low cover, so that would be it. The following night other planes would be out of commission so maybe the Marines would be flying high and the New Zealand fighters flying low and so on. It was a different setup every day.

Q: You really did make your plans day to day.

van Deurs: Oh, they would plan that every night, setup the next day's operation, and of course there were certain planes that had to defend the fields and so on. But that was a day to day operation, and a mixed staff that ran it, and they were backed up by the team that I was with.

Q: Where was Halsey at this point?

van Deurs: Halsey's headquarters was down at Noumea. He was running the whole show down there, ships and everything else.

Q: What was he aboard?

van Deurs: He was on the beach; he wasn't on a ship. He had his quarters at Noumea. He had an advance headquarters up at Guadalcanal and he'd come up and spend quite a bit of time there with a skeleton staff. The communications had gotten so complicated, they'd built a tremendous big radio outfit at Noumea and they couldn't move it, didn't dare put it out of commission long enough to move the darned thing, so he was kind of tied to that. Even when we got up all the way up the line, when operations were heavy, he'd move into his advance headquarters at Guadalcanal or further up, but most of the time he was in Noumea. A lot of the time when things got crossed up or the planning got tangled, I was the guy with the briefcase that got an airplane down to Noumea and talked to his planners and straightened things out.

But to go back to the circles on the chart -- I showed that to Fitch and he was tickled to death. He said, "Get it to Halsey fast, this is the first real planning we've had." Actually that start was sort of the basis for the campaign from there on.

Q: The campaign up the Solomons?

van Deurs: Yes. Except I wanted to go from Munda right to the Treasury Islands, but Vella LaVella looked easy. The Japs were using it as a staging base for barges that were reinforcing people that were still holding on around Munda. I said, "We don't need it, we can reach further than that up to the next field."

But they had the stuff and they decided to take it, and did. It wasn't much of a scrap. There were only a few Japs there — got them, put in a field. It never was used very much.

The circle, the fighter radius, was the determining thing.

There was always an argument about how to name fields. I wanted to keep out of that, so when I laid this thing out I had Field A and Field B and so on. They'd named Henderson Field and Carney Field on Guadalcanal after a couple of people that had got it early in the game and so on, and that left things open on my plans for somebody to put names on them, but nobody ever did.

They got up to Bougainville. We laid out a plan to build three fields inside a perimeter. We didn't want to take all of Bougainville. It was supposed to have about twenty thousand Japs on it. It was a very big island with a mountain range down the middle of it full of volcanoes. Empress Augusta Bay was picked as being remote from any town or anything, where the Japs would have to cut trails through the jungle for miles to come at us. It was laid out, and we had a perimeter, I think it was about three miles in radius, held by the troops, and inside that perimeter we would build three airfields.

There was a point near there called Piva, I think, and I put them on my map as Piva I, Piva II, and Piva III, and damned if the names didn't stick. They all were called that. I thought it showed very little imagination.

Q: Who did the planning, between you and the Navy, for the various naval engagements that took place going up the Solomons?

van Deurs: The ship engagements were run indirectly or directly by Halsey. He had two cruiser divisions at the time and two squadrons of destroyers. The Japanese had been reduced by that time to making night runs down from Bougainville to reinforce their positions, so that one cruiser division and one squadron of destroyers would go up at night to try to intercept these people that were coming down. When they ran out of ammunition, they'd come back to Espiritu Santo to replenish, and the other team would go up. The usual signal was, "The Tokyo Express will run tonight, get 'em."

Q: You did not coordinate with Halsey's planners?

van Deurs: Oh, yes, very much so. That's what I say - I was the briefcase boy.

Q: That's what I wanted you to explain further.

van Deurs: That was mostly on planning the assaults in the landings and the air part of it. The cruiser business just went on as a regular routine. It happened almost every night for months there. Then we had PT boats on Florida Island and Black Cats on Guadalcanal, which were Catalina amphibians that were painted black and specially trained for night work, and they went barge hunting.

The Japanese would follow the coasts and hide out in little inlets and so on. The PT boats and the Catalinas would hunt barges every night all the way up to Bougainville and beyond. Two or three times they got tangled up.

An officer named Bill Specht showed up in my office on Guadalcanal one day - that was after we'd moved up there. Bill had been one of my favorite drinking companions years before in Coronado, and before that a famous football player. Bill was commanding the PT boats operating from Florida Island. He came in - "God damn it, how about getting your Black Cats off my boys' necks?"

We talked it over and we finally made a deal where all the Black Cat pilots spent a night riding the PT boats and vice versa, and then we put them both on the same radio frequency. Well, from then on it was, "Hey, Bill, I think one just went up that creek, (so and so) can you flush him out for me?" And the Black Cat, "Yeah, Jim, I'll get him."

Q: That was wonderful. Was that your idea?

van Deurs: It was one that Bill and I worked out together.

It had a funny angle. Bill said he'd come over in a PT boat from Florida and had to get right back. I said, "Oh, gee, haven't seen you for a long time, have dinner with us and spend the night. There's another cot down in my hut." Finally talked him into it.

He said, "But I have a conference first thing in the morning." I said, "Oh, I'll send you over there in a plane, only take a few minutes for an amphibian plane." Talked him into it.

The next morning the front had moved in and it was raining like somebody'd turned on all the fire hoses in the world, and you couldn't get a plane in the air for anybody. Bill radioed for one of his PTs and left cussing me for a Judas. I've never seen him since, but the scheme worked fine.

Q: I'd think it would.

van Deurs: They had the same trouble with submarines. There were submarines working from Australia that had a habit of running on the surface at night in the passages between Bougainville and Rabaul We didn't know it. We got an Army squadron out there, (This was after we'd gone beyond Munda aways.) got an Army squadron of bombers that were fitted with the first radar bomb sights. They didn't like to fly in the daylight where fighters could get at them, but they loved a dark and stormy night. So we told them they could go up into this area around Rabaul and bomb anything they saw on the surface up there. So they damaged a couple of our submarines that were trying to run through there on the surface in a dark and stormy night.

Q: Did they sink any of them?

van Deurs: I don't think they sank any; I think they batted a couple of them.

Q: Did the submarines know what was hitting them?

van Deurs: They figured it out, because Commodore Fife came tearing over from Australia for a conference, and then we discovered that there was no possible way for a submarine to talk to an airplane. The radio sets were just different. We had some spare airplane radio sets by that time, so we made a deal with Fife that boats going through that area for patrols would stop at Florida Island and we'd put the radio air set on it, install it, and give them the frequencies, and we also gave them an airplane call so the Japs couldn't realize they were hearing submarines. We had a Navy squadron that was running long-range searches to the north all the time, watching for the Jap Fleet to come out of Truk, and these submarines were hunting up in that same area, some of them, so that worked. Where the submarine would sight a ship that it couldn't catch - it was going too fast or going the wrong way - he'd stick his antenna up and call any patrol plane that was around, tell him where it was, and the patrol plane would go bomb it. Vice versa - the patrol plane would see a ship that he couldn't reach, that was beyond his range, he'd open up and use some of these trick calls that would raise a submarine and tip him off that there was a target over there. So that worked out very well.

Q: It was a routine Navy operation in trying to intercept the Japs that were replenishing their remaining garrisons that caused the battle of Kula Gulf and Vella LaVella and so on?

van Deurs: All those things.

Tip Merrill was the Admiral in command of one of those cruiser-destroyer groups, and Pug Ainsworth was the other one. Arleigh Burke got famous as one of the destroyer squadron commanders. The other squadron commander was Roger Simpson, in my class.

Roger, I think, had been passed over one more time than I had as a lieutenant, but he ended up as a commodore at the end of the war. He pulled one down there that was a honey.

We got some carriers down there for a while just before the Central Pacific campaign started, and up at the north end of New Ireland, where we couldn't reach it with the land based air, was the harbor of Kavieng. The Japs used it pretty heavily, with merchant ships and cruisers both. Carriers had raided it once or twice The harbor had two entrances. The planes had to come in from the east, the shipping in there would take-off out the back door and most of it got away. So they set up an operation, with two carriers go up there, I believe, either Christmas or New Year's day. In the meantime they sent Roger Simpson with his destroyers on a big long end run way to the north, way around on the back side of New Ireland to come up towards the back door of Kavieng just as the airplanes hit, and they had quite a harvest as I remember it. The planes got some and some of them ran out the back door and they ran into the destroyers' torpedoes -- very successful.

Then, instead of coming home by the long way around, Roger decided to come home past Rabaul. If you remember the map, there's just a narrow passage between New Ireland and New Britain. The harbor of Rabaul opens off that passage. It's the crater of an extinct volcano where one side's fallen in to make an entrance to the harbor.

By that time we'd been bombing them pretty regularly and they'd put in a lot of guns there, anti-aircraft and dual purpose things, and their gunners had had a lot of practice. They were pretty good.

Roger came through that narrow passage at night. We thought it was probably mined; we didn't know, probably it wasn't. Roger came through there leading the squadron single file, at high speed, went inside the harbor of Rabaul and circled it, with all his guns going, sank everything in the place, and got out.

Q: Who had planned that operation?

van Deurs: He decided that part of it, yes. The Kavieng part of it was a set up deal, but I think going inside of Rabaul was Roger's idea.

Q: A kind of a hazardous venture, wasn't it?

van Deurs: Yeah, but it worked.

Q: Did you find this experience extremely interesting?

van Deurs: Let's say it kept me busy.

Along, I don't know, maybe, as soon as they took Munda practically, they moved ComAir Solomon's headquarters to Munda. And we'd moved from Espiritu Santo up to Guadalcanal and ComAirSol's job was a pretty demanding twenty-four hours a day operation, so that they only kept a man there two or three months, and they rotated things between an Army General, a Navy Admiral, a Marine General, and so on.

At the time they moved to Munda, the Marine had taken over as the boss man, and he asked Moebus to go as his Chief of Staff up there, so I flighted up to Fitch's Chief of Staff when we moved to Guadalcanal. And Al Morehouse came along and took over the planning set up from me.

It kept on being very interesting because that was when it started rolling, and we went on to Vella LaVella, and then the Bougainville operation, and built up that place.

Q: You also acted for Admiral Fitch, didn't you? When he was gone?

van Deurs: Oh yes, but that wasn't very often.

In Espiritu, I mentioned that I got the malaria when I first went out there. Fitch went down to Australia for something, and Moebus was called down to Noumea, and I was the next bird. I was holding the fort at Espiritu for, I don't know, ten days. And I began to feel lousy. I knew I was running a fever, and my old friend Dr. DeFoney was the staff doctor, and also Halsey's malaria control officer, but he was off on a trip somewhere. They had a little doctor running the dispensary there, I've forgotten his name, a little two stripe reserve doctor. I called him and said, "Doc, I feel lousy and I can't quit, I've got to keep on the job." I think the next senior man was a reserve lieutenant or something. "Fix me up someh

"Well," he said, "I don't know what's the matter."

"Find out, for Christ's sake. Do something."

"Well, maybe you've got malaria."

I said, "Maybe I have, but do something."

So he took some blood samples and shoved off. The next day about noon I was sitting over in my hut just holding my head, talking to a man who'd flown a good many hundred miles to get some answers about things. I was trying to make sense, and not too sure I was doing it, just feeling miserable.

Somebody knocked on the door, and this little doc stuck his head in. "I just came to tell you there's nothing wrong with you."

"What the hell do you mean? I'm dying."

"Well, you haven't got malaria."

"I've got something else, then."

"I don't know what it could be."

"Well, find out. Do something anyway."

Went on with the thing. I don't know, maybe a week later Fish got back. Doc DeFoney got back about the same time, and I grabbed him and told him what had happened. He went tearing off and said, "Well, the damn fool had sense enough to send one of those slides down to the malaria lab at the other end of the island. You've got it and you've got it bad. Send you to the hospital."

"What the hell, you can't ---" I'd seen the base hospital. It was a bunch of huts in the mud. I finally talked him into treating it there in camp. He made me swear I'd stay quiet as long as he said to. Took a couple of weeks, I guess.

In the middle of it along came a dispatch making me a captain if I passed the physical exam. I said, "Doc, what are we going to do about that?" "Well, I can't do that, you've got to go to the hospital for a physical exam."

The first day they let me out of the bunk I trotted over to the hospital. The people went over me. Told me they couldn't find any blood pressure, said, "What the hell have you been doing?"

"Well," I said, "this is the first day I've been on my feet - malaria." They finally passed me, let it go, said I'd live. It was kind of a mad tendays before Moebus and DeFoney returned.

Q: Oh, it must have been horrible.

van Deurs: I had two or three kind of unpleasant jobs. Something went wrong, once on Vella LaVella and after Bougainville we went on and took two more islands - Green Island and Emarau - and the word came back that the base commander and the airfield commander were having a big battle on Vella LaVella. The base commander said the airfield commander was drunk all the time, and didn't know his stuff and so on and so forth. Fitch put me in an airplane to go see what the trouble was. The airfield commander had been the air officer in the SARA the second year I was in her, and was passed over for commander, I guess. He was still a lieutenant commander, nice chap, but sort of an old timer. It was kind of embarrassing. I got that straightened out and got back.

Then something of the same kind happened up on Green Island, and I thought - well, I'll have some fun this time. I took a dive bomber and flew to Bougainville, just in time to spend the night with my brother-in-law and have time for a visit. I hadn't realized there was a change of command coming up. An Army General was relieving the Marine General and a lot of the Marines on the staff were due to go home. They'd been out there long enough. Fish was staying over as Chief of Staff for the Army man.

The General sent for us before dinner. We had a couple of drinks together and went into the mess. The camp at Bougainville, the whole place, was within artillery range of the Japs in the jungle. They took guns apart, lugged them on men's back apparently up trails and set them up in the jungle. The jungle was so darned thick we couldn't see where they were, even from planes flying at treetop level. This was Bougainville, outside the perimeter. Every once in a while one of them would open up and begin dropping shells into one of the camps or one of the air strips. We kept a plane flying low over the jungle all day trying to spot them, but their powder was smokeless enough so that nobody could see where these shells were coming from. To counter it, the Army had massed a whole lot more artillery than ordinarily went with the number of troops that were holding the perimeter. When the Jap shells began landing, somebody would run out and look at the hole and say, "It came from over in that direction," and pass the word, and these guns would open up and just rake the jungle back and forth in that direction until the Jap gun quit shooting.

A couple of days later they'd get things fixed up and do it again.

So the place at night was practically blacked out, and naturally the men had shaded lights on the table, part of the greyout or blackout. Some of the Marines who were going home the next day discovered a case of champagne. That helped the party along. Somebody else found some bottles of brandy that helped it along. By the time dinner was over I was feeling no pain. They had put a cot in Moebus' hut for me, and we started over there, fumbling along in the dark. I didn't know my way. He said, "Oh, wait a minute, the guy that lives here is going out tomorrow. I want to say goodbye," so we stuck our heads in there — "Have a drink. We finally got out of there, and the next hut —— "Oh, I want to see those guys." After two or three of those I said, "I can't do any more of this, I have to fly to Green Island in the morning, I'm going to go to sleep." I went on and found the cot.

About two o'clock in the morning I woke up with a terrific head, and looked over at the other cot and Fish was out cold. I started fumbling around looking for the aspirin or anything he might have that would help, and I couldn't find any. I sat down on the edge of the cot holding my head. And all of a sudden there were a lot of flashes outside. I looked out and Jap shells were landing in an open place between a bunch of the huts there. I saw people running for foxholes, but I felt too bad to run; I sat there. I looked over at Fish and he hadn't moved; he hadn't heard a thing.

Then our guns began answering, and I hadn't realized till then that they were all right behind this hut. I don't know how many there were, but they all began shooting at once and then the gunners began playing tricks with their lanyards. They'd go, "Roottitoot, boom boom, rootititoot, boom boom," down the line. And I thought the top of my head was coming off. I'd never had anyhing that hurt so much. This was just the end, but it wasn't ...

Bougainville had a flock of smoking volcanoes, and about that time one of the better earthquakes came along, and this hut just weaved like a blooming flag. And my dear brother-in-law slept through it all; he never moved. The next morning he wouldn't believe it till we got to breakfast and everybody was talking about both the earthquake and the shooting.

When I came back from Green Island I didn't stop to spend the night. I couldn't take two of those.

Q: You had some citations which I haven't seen displayed here - The Legion of Merit. May I read it?

van Deurs: Oh, that was just for being there.

Q: It says, "For exceptional meritorious conduct in the performance of outstanding services, as Plans Officer, Chief of Staff for Commander Aircraft Southern Pacific Force, May 21, '43 to April '44." Continues on, "You capably supervised the preparation of master plan for air operations in the New Georgia area and for the development of air bases at Vella La Vella and Treasury Island, prepared the preliminary air plans for the occupation and development of the Empress Augusta Bay area on Bougainville," and it goes on to say that you sometimes acted when the commander was absent.

Then the Order of The British Empire cites you "for your contributions to the successful operations in New Georgia and Bougainville, and active interest in the Royal New Zealand Air Force of Number one island group, and particularly in his advanced planning of its deployment in new and forward locations. Problems were considerably eased, thus facilitating the maximum operational efficiency under exceptionally difficult conditions."

I was wondering what that refers to ...

van DEurs: The New Zealanders are great people. They're number one fighters. They operated with the airplanes that the Army called obsolete. In other words, they got the leftovers. But whenever there was a scrap they got their share of jobs. They got as many as anybody else did. They had a camp not far from ours on Guadalcan

About once a week maybe the Air Commodore and his number two would come wandering over to see the Admiral, and they'd usually stop in my little office and have a cup of coffee, and I'd take them in to see the old man. There was always this conversation about, "Why can't we have coffee as good as this over in our mess?" They were getting the same ration from the Army quartermaster that we wer They'd pinched a silex just like we had. "Doesn't taste the same."

I finally asked them one day how they made tea, and I got a long lecture on how to heat the teapot and what the teapot should be made of and the temperature of this and the duration of that, and -- very elaborate.

I said, "How do you make coffee?" He said, "You take a stew pot and throw some coffee in it and boil it up."

I said, "Well, if you'd take as much trouble with it as you do with your tea, it would taste the same as ours."

But every once in a while those two birds would come walking in -- could they have a cup of coffee? No, thanks. Didn't have anything to say, and looked kind of sour. I'd take them in to see the old man. It would turn out they'd heard a rumor we were going to move somebody up further forward, and they were going to be left out, and they didn't want to be left out of any fighting. We'd smooth that over and then everything was rosy again. But the only kick they ever had was that they might get left out of some shooting.

Q: Is that what it refers to where it says, "facilitated the maximum operational efficiency under exceptionally difficult conditions?"

van Deurs: I guess so.

But that was the only kick they ever had, and they were a jolly good bunch.

Q: But they were one of the various groups that were all under the same command.

van Deurs: Yes, they were under Fitch the same as the Army Air Force, Marine Air, and so forth.

That citation actually was presented in Washington after the war was over when I was in the Navy Department.

Q: The Legion of Merit or the citation?

van Deurs: The British Empire thing.

Q: The Order of The British Empire, Honorary Commander.

van Deurs: That Legion of Merit was hung on me at Guadalcanal, actually by the Marine General that had been on Bougainville.

Q: First they were on Munda, then they went to Bougainville?

van Deurs: Yes, they moved first to Munda and then moved on to Bougainville.

I guess before the South Pacific campaign was quite finished they ordered Fitch back to the Navy Department as Chief of Bureau of Aeronautics, or DCNO Air, I've forgotten which, and Ralph Mitchell the Marine General, took over as Commander Air South Pacific. I stayed as his Chief of Staff I guess until we closed up the job.

Q: But actually you made your own plans. You got there at the time when there were no plans, and based on your own knowledge and interviews and research, you actually, with the conditions that were then existing and almost without guidance, prepared these yourself?

van Deurs: I came close enough to preparing them so that Fitch and Halsey accepted them, and I went on from there.

Q: Did you get guidance from them?

van Deurs: No, because up to that time there hadn't been much planning. Some way or other they were going to get to Rabaul - that was the idea.

That's the way it works. The staff is supposed to work things out, and if they work it out right then the Old Man adopted it as his idea and fights for it. Fitch was very good at that. He wasn't a particularly brilliant man, but he had the knack of taking people that disagreed violently and didn't like each other - Fitch could make them work in double harness and like it. That was his valuable point. He never did any planning.

The staff would work up something, either me or Al Morehouse and I together maybe, and present it to him, and hewent ahead with criticism, would object to this, that, or the other point. We'd work that out and then he'd say, "All right, this is the team proposal. This is my idea." He'd take it to Halsey. That was what he wanted to do, and he'd fight for it.

Q: But all you knew was your goal was Rabaul, and it was your plans on how to get there.

van Deurs: Yes, that's what it amounted to.

It was funny, before one of these amphibious operations, Halsey was in Noumea. On Guadalcanal with us was the amphibious commander, and often the head Marine or Army General. So Halsey's planners down south would say, "We want to go to Vella La Vella," for instance, and ask Fitch, "Sound out the people at Guadalcanal on the best way to do it."

So Fitch would call a conference of Admiral Wilkinson, the amphibious guy, and maybe Marine Air, or the Marine General who was going to be in it, and everybody conerned. Before that conference would be called he'd have his own staff work up a plan that he thought would work for it, and maybe change it, maybe not, but he'd get it so that he'd put it in his pocket and say that was the staff' solution, that was his plan.

I usually sat in the background with nothing to say on these conferences. They all would start out the same way. They'd go round the room and everyone of these big shots would have an entirel different idea. Jakie Fitch would explain the problem - we have to do this. Each one had a completely divergent idea how to do it, and they'd talk it over and talk it around and toss it back and fort till they finally got somewhere near agreement, and Fitch would kind of sum it up and say, "Well, I've got the opinion -- we'll do this, that, and the other, ABC. Is that right, Joe?" And Joe'd say, "Yes, that's fine," and right around. Usually it would suit everybody till he came to General Geiger, the Marine. And Geiger always made me think of a fat Buddha. He'd be sitting there with a big gri on his face. "Have you fellows thought what would happen if - so and so?" and he'd have a point, a good one, that nobody had thought Well, that would throw them all into confusions again. This argumer would go round again. Maybe it would happen a couple of times. It was always Geiger who threw the monkey wrench into the agreement.

Q: He was the Devil's advocate?

van Deurs: He was a very good Marine, good aviator.

But when we got through with the thing without knowing it they'd usually agreed on practically the staff solution that Jakie had in his pocket. And they all went away happy thinking that their plan had been accepted.

Q: That's a wonderful man.

van Deurs: That was Fitch's genius. I used to sit there and wonder how he did it. I saw it happen a half a dozen times, and I never quite figured out how he made it work, but he always did. He said very little and everybody went away convinced that they'd sold the Old Man on their plans.

The staff worked a lot harder than he did, but as Fish explained when I first went down there, "Part of our job is to take the load off the Old Man. He's pretty close to sixty years old and is extremely valuable because he can make people work together, and we don't want him to wear out, so you don't bother him unless you have to.

On Guadalcanal he had a cabin. It was a fancied up quonset hut, right next to it was a little Dallas hut that I used as an office, with a Marine orderly between the two. Fitch used to hold a cocktail hour for the staff every afternoon. In the back of his cabin we had a little bar and kept a liquor mess in there, and about an hour before supper people would begin to wander in and pour themselves whatever they wanted, and tell dirty stories, or play practical jokes, or do anything else to quit thinking about the war for an hour or so. It was just his way of kind of relieving the tension, and it was a very good performance. We would have a couple of snorts and go in to dinner.

I found that I always left a stack of urgent things on my desk, dispatches and letters, that had to be either farmed out or corrected or what have you, decisions, and I always tried to take the Old Man a solution, not a problem. I found that if I got up from dinner and went back to the office, that six guys would follow me in with their problems; and I'd never get to my own.

On a side hill by the mess we had a little coconut log theater laid out, a movie amphitheatre, and the movies were usually terrible but I'd go out there and light a cigar, get the thing started, and as soon as it got well started I'd sneak out and go back to the office and get things done.

Fitch sometimes went to the movies. He couldn't read at night; the light in his cabin wasn't any good he said, so by nine o'clock he was pounding his ear. About midnight or later I'd quit, go down to my little hut on the edge of the hill and turn in. Maybe I'd get called two or three times in the night with some telegram that came in. I either batted them or sent them on to the Old Man. I don't think there were more than one or two cases where I figured it was worth waking him up.

Anyway about five o'clock in the morning he was wide awake, and the chief steward would be in there at five o'clock with a cup of coffee. The Old Man would get up and take a long walk around the place, and then at seven o'clock, when our mess hall opened, he'd be the first one in there, starved to death. It was the middle of his morning and he was ready to do business. Somewhere in between he'd read all the telegrams that came in during the night and he wanted somebody to talk to about them.

So about seven the boy would call me with a cup of coffee and the Marine would bring in everything that I hadn't seen during the night, and I'd get a shower and try to open my eyes with the coffee and go through these dispatches, knowing the minute I walked in to breakfast the Old Man would want to talk about them.

"Van, did you see the one from Halsey about so and so?" I would tell him I had done so and so. "What do you think we ought to do about thus and so?" It began right there before I got my breakfast ordered. It never hit him that ...

Q: You might have been up half the night?

van Deurs: No, he never discovered that.

But it was the middle of the morning to him. He was just lonesome, waiting for somebody to talk to. I had to be primed before I could go in for breakfast. But he was a great man to work for. I appreciated him. He was very nice.

Q: Are we almost to the next segment?

I was wondering if we should quit now and take it up tomorrow.

Interview # 4

Interview with Admiral George van Deurs
San Francisco
October 12, 1969
by E. B. Kitchen

Admiral van Deurs: We were in the Solomons for something over a year. I got a message from Moebus, who was up on Bougainville by that time, enclosing a set of leave papers, asking me to get the Admiral to sign them, giving him a week's leave. There was a note with it, to go around also and talk with the head man of the 13th Air Force and see if I could get some leave papers signed for Brigadier Metheney. Metheney was the Army officer in charge of the bomber command, heavy bombers, and relations were a little bit strained with his boss so he wanted me as intermediary. Fish said, "If Metheney can get his papers signed, we'll take one of his bomber and we will fly direct to Sidney."

So I got Metheney's papers fixed up and then I took Fish's in to Admiral Fitch and said, "My brother-in-law wants me to get you to sign these." Fitch said, "Sure."

"Admiral, that's wrong," I said, "you know that guy can't be trusted. You can't send him down to Sidney without somebody to watch him." "Why don't you go watch him?" I said, "I hoped that's what you'd say," and plopped my leave papers in front of him.

So these two took a B-24, came down to Guadalcanal, picked me up, and we flew direct to Sidney for a week. It was quite a welcome change after a year in the islands. We got quite a bit of fun out of it.

Part of it was, Fish and I rented a flat for some exorbitant price for the duration, and went shopping for chow in delicatessen and green grocer's shops. Everything looked so good — we hadn't seen any fresh food for a year, and the poor gal that was running this green grocery shop thought us mad. "We want some of those, some of those, and some of this." She finally decided that nobody was going to pay for all that stuff, but we got it, and we enjoyed it. It was quite a leave.

Part of the deal was to load the airplane up with liquor to take back to one of the messes up there. We couldn't buy any liquor in Sidney. So instead of going directly home we flew over to New Zealand and spent one night in Aukland, and managed to buy several cases of whiskey there to put in the B-24, and then back to Guadalcanal.

The Air Force wanted fresh food for their pilots, particularly eggs, and regularly sent a plane to New Zealand or Australia to come back with a cargo of fresh eggs. There was one mountain on the end of Guadalcanal that Metheney used to point out, "There's my $40,000 omelet." One of the planes loaded with eggs had flown into the mountain and splashed everything.

There were humorous things like that that happened all along to many of us.

Most people who got some leave wanted to do what we did -- go down to Sidney and see some city life, some drinking, and so on -- not so, General Mitchell. After he was up on Bougainville, they offered him some leave, and he went down to New Zealand. He'd heard of their fabulous trout fishing. He spent his leave fishing.

In New Zealand there were no fresh water fish when the white people first went there. They imported rainbow trout from California and planted them in the streams. They grew to be the size of salmon, with no natural enemies, and apparently the fishing is famous. There were all kinds of fishing resorts. These hotels were all equipped for fishermen, but there were no fishermen during the war. Mitchell was the only one they'd seen in a couple of years. He had the places to himself. He had some trout smoked, packed in dry ice, and shipped it back to Guadalcanal for the mess. It was the best thing I tasted during the war.

It was a small and select cocktail party on Guadalcanal one day - the General in charge of Marine Air was out there from Washington, and Geiger was there commanding a Marine division, and Nutts Moore was given his second star, Major General, and they had this little cocktail party to celebrate it. Someone looked around and said, "Hey, there are five Marine Major Generals here wearing wings. That's the first time it ever happened in history. In fact, it's the first time there have even been five Marine Major Generals that were aviators." One of them, Pat Mulcahy, spoke up and said, "Yeah, it's the first time in a hell of a lot of years that all five of them have been speaking to each other, too."

I spent a couple of months as Chief of Staff for General Mitchell ...

Q: That was after Bristol?

van Deurs: After Fitch left.

Marines were always putting up a solid united front against the Navy or anybody outside the Corps. But working for Mitchell gave me kind of a peak inside the Marine Corps, and I discovered that there half a dozen people, Marines, on Guadalcanal that were all trying to cut each other's throat and all of them trying to see Mitchell, trying to enlist him on their side of the political thing. There were more internal politics in the Marine Corps than any place I ever saw, but it was always under cover. Unless you were a Marine you didn't know it was going on. I imagine it still exists. It certainly wasn't new. Some of them I discovered were feuds that had been going on for years.

In June of '44 they decided to close up the Solomon operation. Bougainville was on MacArthur's side of the line anyway. They left some troops to hold that and left a Marine Air Wing there, and turned the area over to - I don't know who, I guess maybe somebody on MacArthur's team. It was dead, it was finished. Halsey went to command the Third Fleet. The rest of the commands were being broken up.

Fitch, back in Washington, wrote both Fish and me and asked us what we wanted to do. We both said we wanted a flat top. As a joke we said, "We'll settle for the SARATOGA because she's the biggest."

We got orders back to the States for re-assignment, and it looked perfect. I got relieved, turned over to whoever was taking over what was left of my job, waited a day for Fish to come down from Bougainville so we could travel together. We were all setup with number one air priority to the States, baggage all packed up, plane going out at six o'clock in the evening from Henderson Field, and we started taking a sunbath alongside of my hut. Swede Ekstrom came along and said, "What the hell are you doing here?" We smugly said, "We're going home tonight, ha ha ha, we're all setup."

But we were lying there worrying. We had an awful lot of baggage. We were overweight. We knew we'd get out of Henderson all right because we'd been running the place, but we weren't sure about Pearl, and there were some nasty rumors that people coming out of the South Pacific got as far as Pearl and were being turned around and sent somewhere in the Central Pacific. We both sort of wanted some leave.

Swede said, "Oh, I'm going home too. I got a carrier down at the dock loaded with old Army planes. I've got orders to take them right to San Diego nonstop. Why don't you go with me?" He said, "I'm all filled up with passengers, but I'll be using the sea cabin, and if one of you guys will sleep on the cot you can have the cabin."

Well, we thought that over a minute and thought about overnight stops on coconut islands full of mosquitoes, and getting up early, and having the plane not work. We said, "We'll take you."

The people who wrote the orders were right across the road. I took our orders over there and said, "Hey, scratch the 'air' off of here and put first available government transportation, instead of first available air." They thought I was nuts because everybody was fighting for air transport.

The colored boy, a very black chief steward, that had been my boy for a long time, and before that he'd been Fish's, came along and asked, "Do you gentlemen need anybody to carry your bags this eveni

We got thinking about it. He was an awfully decent guy, and had been a survivor off a ship, and had been down there longer than either of us. So we went back across the street and asked if they could write some orders for an enlisted man for the States. No, they couldn't do that, but they had orders to keep the carriers filled up. They wrote orders for this chap to Swede's carrier.

We went back, "Baker, if you had some orders for the States, could you be ready to go in half an hour?" He moved into the captain's pantry and paid off by making pie every day all the way home.

Over at Nandi in the Fijis we had an air strip. The Army lived on one side of it, and the Navy camped on the other side. The Navy camp was commanded by a Chester Bates, who had been an aviator in World War I and came back as a Reserve Lieutenant Commander. In between he was a cotton buyer and apparently a very good one and very prosperous at it - some firm up in New England, I think. He was also one of the craziest white men I'd ever met.

The first time I went to Nandi on an inspection trip, he was showing us around. Here were a couple of airplanes sitting on the line that didn't have any number on them. Well, they had this repair crew there, they had to have something to practice on, so they had taken a couple of wrecks off the scrap heap and built airplanes, perfectly good flying machines. His crew had a beautiful big concrete handball court, concrete walks all around the quonset huts. I said, "Where the hell did you get all this concrete?" Cement was one of the things that was scarcer than gold dust in the Solomons.

"Stole it from the Army. Some day the General will figure out where it is, he'll come and accuse me of stealing it. I'll say, 'Sure, I've got your cement, help yourself.'"

When the heat was on, the bird was a wonderful leader. When it wasn't on he had to have something to amuse himself, and deviling the Army General in command of the islands over there was his favorite. The General had commandeered a lot of the lumber consigned to Chet. The Army didn't have any and the General just took this lumber, so Chet swore a vendetta, he was going to get even.

When the General threatened him with general court, Chet said, "Come on, I never had a general court. Go on give me one. In fact I'll give you a thousand dollars for one. Here's a check. I'll give you a thousand dollars to give me a general court."

In the early days we had built a field up the island a little ways that had never been used. The war moved on, grass grew up through the Marston mat, and we wanted to know if it was worth salvaging the mat. So Chet drove me up to see it. As we drove along we passed a place where they'd built a dock of coconut logs. A freighter was there unloading lumber, into a long line of trucks, Army trucks. Chet looked till he saw a couple of Navy trucks in the line. He explained, "I called up my Army friend and offered him trucks to help unload this ship, said I had some trucks that weren't working. And if those drivers don't get lost from that convoy coming back, they won't eat for a week."

Sure enough, coming back on a little bit of a side road going like hell was a great big Navy truck piled high with lumber barreling through the jungle.

Next day I looked all around the camp. There wasn't a sign of lumber anywhere. But they had a couple of big quonset huts full of airplane spares, and the lumber that the General had commandeered had been supposed to make a deck and shelving to put this stuff on, instead of just letting it be in the mud. The next day that quonset hut was full of beautiful shelving, and all the stuff was stored on the shelves.

Q: He must have been quite a guy.

van Deurs: Not only quite a guy. He was funny, an ingrown sense of humor, and as men caught onto the thing they enjoyed all the pranks.

He had this Filipino boy Joe that I was a little bit afraid of. I think if Chet had ever told him to shoot somebody Joe would have laughed like hell and pulled the trigger. He was just that loyal. He thought Bates was the funniest man in the world, and he'd do anything Bates wanted, and it didn't make any difference how crazy it was.

Running up and down the side of the field was a great big steamroller painted battleship grey, with USN and a number on it, and it was over on the Army side of the field with a sailor in a white hat running it up and down the edge of the field.

Bates said, "It just seemed like something that was tough to steal. The Army Engineers were building a road near here, using that steamroller. I thought it would be kind of fun to steal the steamroller I never had. So we went out one night, brought it down here and put Navy numbers on it. One of the sailors has been running up and down in front of the Army camp for a week now while the engineers are going nuts hunting all over the island for it. They haven't figured out what happened yet."

He had great fun with Dr. DeFoney on our staff. They'd known each other in the First War. Couple of times Chet Bates came over to our camp for some kind of a conference. First thing would be to insist on bunking with the Doc in his hut. Then he'd steal the Doc's wallet and his watch and everything else he could stuff in his suitcase to get ready to go. We'd have to shake him down upon leaving the place.

We decided he was too good a man to waste on a backwater like Nandi and sent him back to the States to form a new Acorn, or air base unit. Chet asked us to take Joe, his Filipino boy. Joe wanted to get closer to the war. He had only been in California a few month when war broke out. He came from a little village upon Linguayen Gulf, where the Japs landed. He had no idea what happened to the rest of his family, and he wanted to kill Japs. He was pretty mad at being over in the Fijis where there weren't any Japs, and thought he should be a little bit closer. He became Fish's boy when he came over to our place. He adopted Fish, and when Fish went up to Bougainville he took Joe with him. Well, Joe was the number one houseboy during the daytime. He did everything he was supposed to around the camp. But in some way he collected a terrific arsenal of guns and knives and what have you, and as soon as it got dark went hunting Japs.

Q: Out in the jungle, alone?

van Deurs: Yeah. He got mad a couple of times because the Marines shot at him.

The perimeter around Bougainville was a bunch of trenches, we had no intention of going any further. The Japanese made a habit of sending about a battalion against it every night, which was not enough. They'd punch a hole in the perimeter, but the next morning there'd be one more battalion short. On account of those nightly raids, trying to infiltrate, when it got dark along the front every Marine and every soldier crawled in his private little foxhole and shot at anything he heard moving during the night. You just didn't get out of your hole during the night. But little Joe would get up there and try to go through the line.

Joe knew exactly what the score was. He made his expeditions and it made him happy doing it. Before that when we were still on Espiritu Santo he used to go out with Doc DeFoney into the jungle working on mosquito control work, trying to find the places they bred, do something about it. Joe would take a gunny sack along and he'd dig up plants, roots, and things that none of us knew what they were, bring them back to camp, and we'd have new vegetables on the table that night. We never got anything but a Filipino name for them but they all tasted good. He was apparently a pretty good little jungle man.

Q: I thought you were going to say, when you got your trip back with Admiral Ekstrom that he was going with you.

van Deurs: No. Fish got him ordered back to San Deigo ahead of himself.

We got word from Fitch that I was going to get one of the converted tankers, the carrier CHENANGO, and Fish, because he was senior, would get the SARATOGA.

He sent Joe back to San Diego with orders to wait for him and when he got a ship he'd take him with him in the ship. Joe was a pretty tough little nut, very decided on what he wanted, and it was a month or so before Fish got to Coronado. The personnel officer grabbed him with delight because Joe wouldn't do anything. They'd tried to ship him out two or three times, and no sir, he was Captain Moebus's boy and he wasn't going anywhere till Captain Moebus said so. He had the whole personnel outfit down there in an uproar. They were delighted to get rid of him, but the only way they could get rid of him was to find Moebus.

Something else I wanted to tell you ...

Q: Before you got aboard the carrier?

van Deurs: Oh, Bates came back with an Acord, which we didn't need right away, so we staged it ashore on the Russell Islands. That is they piled equipment and gear there and waited. There were two or three other outfits staging there.

Q: He came back while you were still there?

van Deurs: Oh yes, he came back. He formed this outfit at Port Heuneme, and brought it back out. It was probably the best equipped of any of them because having been through it before Bates knew what he'd need in the way of concrete, lumber, tools, all kinds of things, and could really fit himself out.

But there were two or three other outfits staging at the Russell Islands at the same time. It was just a place where they told them to camp until they were needed up the line. It wasn't a week till we had all kinds of commanding officers screaming bloody murder because Chet was stealing this and that and doing all kinds of tricks just for amusement.

About that time we were just going into Bougainville the naval base commander up there kind of fell apart and things weren't going right. So we told Bates to leave his outfit with the executive officer, and sent him up there to command the air strips at Bougainville. Well, he got them into shape in short order, made a swell job of it.

Q: Was he a SeaBee?

van Deurs: No, he wasn't a SeaBee, he was an ex-aviator.
The fields were built, it was the operation that was sour.

Q: That's what I thought, but he was able to do all these things.

van Deurs: It was a case of getting somebody to administer the place and get it organized. As soon as he got it running we began getting pleas from the Generals up there to get him out of their hair. He was going wild in Bougainville again.

One day after we were living here in Belvedere the telephone rang. A voice said, - it was for Admiral van Deurs - "Are you the son-of-a-bitch who was down in Bougainville?" It was Chet Bates.

He was living over in Sausalito, and having a bad time. Apparently in the cotton buying business, the trick was to be able to feel a cotton sample between the thumb and the forefinger and judge the grade right now. And he had had the magic thumb. But in an accident he'd lost his thumb, and it put him out of the cotton business. He was still a hustler. He worked for some of the shipping companies that I knew here, rounding up cargo and stealing cargo from other lines and having himself a big time, all the way from here to Lower California, but he died about two years ago, still going on.

Q: He must have had a good time with his life, didn't he.

van Deurs: At Nandi I saw, on his desk, checks for $20,000 and things like that, just lying around with a bunch of papers. Can't do anything with it here, just throw it in the pile - profit from the cotton firm.

And the amazing part there was a very quiet little officer on Halsey's staff, one of the intelligence crew, that I found out was one of Bates' partners in the cotton business. Lawyer, very quiet and dignified sort of a kid and quite a bit younger than Bates. Every time I'd go down there he'd ask me if I'd seen Bates and how he was doing, and the other way around. Finally I asked this kid how he happened to get mixed up with a crazy guy like Bates. "Oh," he said, "Bates started out as my father's partner." He said he got out of law school and hung up a shingle in New York, started law practice, but he was always getting busted out in the middle of the night by a telephone. Bates would be down in Texas or Georgia or somewhere, "Hey, Johnny, I just did so and so, and you've got to get me out of jail, they're after me."

He said, "I spent so much time getting Bates out of one scrape after another that I gave up trying to practice and went with the firm as a full time job of keeping Bates out of trouble."

Halsey had his advance headquarters at Guadalcanal. The dividing line between Nimitz' territory and MacArthur's was just at the end of Guadalcanal, so each operation we did on up the Solomons had to be okayed by MacArthur before we could do them. Mick Carney, Halsey's Chief of Staff, and some helpers were over in Brisbane trying to get agreement on a plan for the next operation - I've forgotten what it was now, up the line somewhere. Halsey wanted to get some word to Carney, but he didn't want to put it on the radio in a code that MacArthur could read, and so he grabbed me and told me to go to Brisbane, fly over there, find Carney and to tell him thus and so, which I did.

I thought I'd be coming right back -- maybe had a spare shirt, but not much more. Carney said, "Stick around a few days, things aren't going the way they ought to, and I may want you to take some word back to the Old Man. Anyway, you might find it interesting."

We were all quartered in the only decent hotel in Brisbane, a modern building, the only modern building in town, that MacArthur had taken over. He lived in a penthouse up on the roof, and his staff and so on occupied the rest of it. There was a side entrance to the place for apartments, and Admiral Kinkaid had an apartment up there.

I played along, to see Brisbane for a couple of days - when all of a sudden a lot of us, including me, were presented with an invitation to a formal dinner, at six-thirty or seven o'clock, on account of Admiral Nimitz had arrived. It was the first time the two of them had met. Nimitz had flown down apparently to try to smooth things over in a political way. I couldn't figure why I was included.

By that time the Khaki I'd flown over in was looking pretty crumby. Admiral Kinkaid took pity on that. He had a couple of Chinese boys who'd escaped from the Philippines. For a wonder - they put me in one of the Admiral's bathrobes and took the khaki and made it look like new in about half an hour.

MacArthur was famous for never doing anything social. All Brisbane was yak-yaking about this thing because all the time he'd been there he had no social contact with anybody - Australians or anybody else - very much the lone wolf. This was the first time he'd ever entertained at all.

It was also known that he never served liquor, so Carney and the rest of the South Pacific detachment had three or four good snorts before we went down, and we ended up at the tail end of the receiving line, with MacArthur and Nimitz greeting everybody - purely a stag affair.

They had a big U table and a couple of side tables, all with place cards. I found myself isolated with a bunch of Army quartermasters and trasnportation officers - couldn't find any common interest for conversation at all with them.

There were about three stem glasses in front of each place. We looked at those and thought - gee, it's going to be better than we thought, he's going to break out something. Well, they came along and filled the glasses with tomato juice and water and orange juice, or something like that.

Then we were served a GI ration - canned peas and canned meat, or something. It was a very poor meal.

At the top of the U table Nimitz and MacArthur were talking very quietly with each other all during the meal. None of us could figure why we were there except that maybe there was going to be some kind of a speech or announcement by one of them or both of them. But after the chow was finished, the two of them got up and walked out, and everything was all over.

I never could figure out why the dinner party. Nobody said boo, nobody made a speech, nobody said anything. We all filed out of the place and the South Pacific detachment went looking for a bottle, trying to figure out what it was all about. We never did.

Q: What was the conflict that occasioned Nimitz' trip - do you recall?

van Deurs: I haven't any idea what came out of it. Only time I saw Nimitz while he was there was at that dinner party.

Q: I mean - what was the conflict that caused him to go there?

van Deurs: Oh, there'd been a lot of political backbiting and so on. MacArthur had been sneering at the Central Pacific idea. He was trying to force the Joint Chiefs of Staff to let him return to the Philippines, and trying to get the Pacific Fleet put under his command to return him to the Philippines, and that island hopping business was not - he wanted to use carriers for just supporting him Army, just protecting the flank of his Army. The Navy thought they should be used aggressively to attack and advance through the Central Pacific. So there'd been a lot of nasty doubletalk on the thing. Nimitz ran down there to try to smooth it out, personal contact, to try to do a little diplomacy.

Q: Probably did - in MacArthur's book he speaks awfully highly of Nimitz.

van Deurs: Well, before that he was speaking very lowly. He used to say, "Neémitz." So if he speaks highly of him in his book, maybe it was partly the result of that conference.

Q: Nimitz apparently had the characteristic, as you say of Fitch, of getting people to work together.

van Deurs: Yeah, Nimitz was a very smooth man to pull things together. I flew back to Guadalcanal a couple of days later still wondering. One other funny thing ...

Q: You did take the word though from Halsey to Carney and back to Halsey?

van Deurs: Yeá. Well, it was a funny place. We learned that they had this high powered staff there, and the gang hadworked a long time on these plans and they couldn't get a yes or no out of anybody. There wasn't anybody on MacArthur's staff that had thepower to agree to anything.

Q: MacArthur had to make all the decisions.

van Deurs: What we found out was that the plans had to be sent up to New Guinea to General Krueger, who was the man that did MacArthur's fighting. He was the fighting general that was on the front. And if Krueger said okay, then MacArthur would agree. If Krueger didn't, well it was too bad. He depended on Krueger, not on his staff.

While we were sitting around there waiting for the word to come back from Keureger, which is what it amounted to, we were granted an audience with MacArthur. Invited in to talk things over is what it amounted to. He did all the talking, pacing up and down the office, and waving a pipe. He'd do that for a while, never light the pipe, put that pipe down on the desk, and pick up another, and go back to walking and waving that one. When we came out some of his staff said, "Did you get the two, three, or four pipe treatment?"

I don't remember learning anything startling in that conference at all.

Q: But you took back to Halsey the word ...

van Deurs: I've forgotten what it was. It was some minor point.

We were in a peculiar spot down there in the Solomons. There were a lot of reporters on Guadalcanal, but MacArthur insisted that the word had to go out in his communiques, and he'd put out a communique about how his Marines took Munda and his this and his that did something else, which burned up everybody on the Solomons. But the reporters that were there were not allowed to mention anything that hadn't been mentioned in one of MacArthur's communiques, which meant that by the time we'd decoded and read MacArthur's communique anything they sent in was too late to make the deadlines and was old stuff. So they finally worked out a scheme where an intelligence officer on Guadalcanal would say, "We guess that MacArthur will put this, that, and the other thing in his communiques tonight," so the reporters would write their stories about those things. They'd code it and put in on the punch tape for the transmitter and mark the tape that this was a story about this or a story about that. Then they'd wait for the communique. The minute they had it, if it mentioned all those things, they'd put the reporters' tapes in the transmitting machine. If he'd left out one of the items, they'd clip that out of the tape, splice it together, and let it go. That way the boys got some of their stories printed.

But his communiques were horribly distorted all through the war. I came home from Japan with a general that had been one of his intelligence people and asked him about it on the trip - how come they put out so damned many lies. He said that his outfit was giving MacArthur the straight dope, and at first they'd objected to some of these communiques, but they were told that the communique was purely a press relations business, had no connection with intelligence, and they had no business to interfere at all. They couldn't do anything about it. There was no connection between what was going on and what was reported by MacArthur to the press.

All of that made us rather unhappy on the Solomons. We thought we were doing a pretty good job -- but we didn't get any credit.

Q: Fortunately history has told the actual story.

van Deurs: Well, the history will be MacArthur's communiques.

Q: Perhaps our history that we're doing will help to correct it.

van Deurs: One outfit - the carrirs were raiding up by Kavieng. One plane was lost, a torpedo plane. I believe there were two man in it. They got into a rubber boat and floated for about a month. They were pretty well done in, when they drifted onto an atoll way to the north of the Solomons in the Lord Howe group. It was uninhabited, with coconut trees on it, and they managed to subsist on coconuts for maybe another month. And then by chance one of our planes at the far end of a search sighted the islands and sighted a couple of men on the beach and the yellow boat, so a seaplane went up there and brought them back to Bougainville. They'd been gone about two months and weren't in very good shape. We put them in a plane to go down to Guadalcanal and then go on home for treatment.

SCAT, Southern Combat Air Transport, ran a DC-3, inter-island air service. Some of the pilots were not too experienced. The Russell Islands, by that time we had a couple of big airfields on them. One was right across a peninsula, with water at each end. The bird flying this SCAT plane, just for the hell of it, came down and flew down this airstrip about one hundred feet in the air, maybe, just in passing. He wasn't watching his gas tanks, and ran his gas tank dry just about the time he got to the end of the airstrip - crashed on a coral reef. That was obviously the end of the script. Killed everybody on board. It always seemed to me pretty grim, to have survived two months in a rubber boat and a coconut island, be almost home, and get knocked off.

Q: Both of them?

van Deurs: Everybody on the plane was knocked off - plane load of people. The two rubber boat survivors happened to be among them.

Q: Was this pilot just being funny?

van Deurs: Yeah, just kid stuff, and carelessness. Ordinarily you shifted a gas tank, before it ran dry you turned on another tank, but he wasn't watching his stuff.

Q: Isn't that tragic.

van Deurs: Somewhere during the Munda show, I guess, we began having an awful lot of forced landings in the Russells. Planes coming back from all the line were having forced landings on the Russell Island all the time, and then we heard a rumor that there was a hamburger stand on the Russell Islands. Well, fresh meat was something you just didn't have on the Solomon Islands. There wasn't any refrigeration to send it down there for people.

Finally I think Fitch sent me over there to find out what was going on. I landed on one of these strips and as I rolled down the strip right alongside of the strip was a little shack with white oilcloth or white front and and a white roof and a big sign, "Free hamburgers for Pilots." A guy was inside with a white chef's cap and apron. This was really something. Found out he was a SeaBee. I went looking for the boss SeaBee who served me a beautiful steak for lunch.

Q: Sounds like your friend Chester Bates.

van Deurs: Same kind of an operator.

I said, "How come? How does this happen?" Well, he said, they appreciated that the pilots were doing a powerful job for them, fighting, and they thought they'd like some hamburgers, and so they set up a hamburger stand with free hamburgers for pilots.

Q: Where were they getting their meat?

van Deurs: That's what I asked.

The Russell Islands had been almost entirely coconuts before the war, Lever Brothers, and like all the groves had run cattle through them to keep the jungle back. We had very strict orders not to bother the cattle. They were the property of our friends and allied people. The CO said, "You know, it's a strange thing around here, a couple of times we thought we were going to run out of beef, and believe it or not one of these cows attacked a sentry and he had to shoot him in self defense!" It was a good steak.

Q: I think that was a good idea. I'm sorry about the cows, but ...

van Deurs: When they were building the airfields on the Russell Islands they ran into a horrible problem of rain. It rained for forty days, and then some. Washed out everything as fast as they could put it in. We wanted the fields ready by the time we started out for Munda. The time was getting close.

I flew over there in a seaplane with Fitch to see what was going on, and found the base commander and two or three people lined up with jeeps, I guess to take us down to where they were digging. I rode along with the Naval Base Commander. He was a Reserve officer that had worked for me in Corpus Christi. I was glad to see him. This rain was coming down like it was out of a fire hose dripping all over everything. We splashed along through muddy ruts in this jeep, between coconut trees. As far as you could see through the rain there were rotting coconuts all over the ground that had sprouted. They hadn't been harvested for two or three years. As this bird bounced the jeep along he said, "Had a letter from my wife the other day in Detroit. Said she paid nineteen cents for a coconut. Look at the God damned things!" He swept his arm around and we skidded but recovered.

The SeaBees changed their drainage plans and got the field in on time. Then we had pretty good weather in the Russells for a long time.

Q: Those stories are all intriging and certainly make background information.

van Deurs: None of that's history, but ...

Q: It's footnotes to history, I think.

van Deurs: There's quite a little background about the camp down there. The whole thing was a shoestring operation.

People, reporters, called Halsey "Bull," which is a name he never liked. He was Bill Halsey. They had a habit of quoting him out of context, making him look funny. Actually he had the knack of saying something at a time that made men accomplish the impossible, just sort of a feeling. I told you about showing him what the Japs could do to us by air, and we didn't have any way of defending it. "Well, I've got a hunch they aren't going to so we're going anyway."

He could say something that made a bunch of men fight like the dickens and do something that was impossible, and then some reporter would pick it up and quote it out of context and make it sound silly. At the time he said it it was probably the one thing that could be said to make things happen.

Q: He was a great leader.

van Deurs: That was his strong point, he was a personal leader.

I can't give an example right now, except he'd been up I guess on Kolombangara just after we took the place and picked up a bunch of Japanese money, which he pulled out of his pocket and showed me. "What are you going to do with that, spend it in Tokyo?" He said, "When I get to Tokyo I'd not going to pay for a God damned thing!"

Q: Your closest contact with Halsey was during this period?

van Deurs: When he was skipper of the SARATOGA, and during this period in the South Pacific. I never served with him in the Third Fleet. Never had anything to do with him there, but I saw quite a bit of him in the South Pacific.

Q: I was going to ask you before we left this part of your career, about Halsey, so I'm glad ...

van Deurs: I think he was undoubtedly the greatest personal leader. That South Pacific campaign was entirely Halsey's personality. A handful of Marines and soldiers and aviators licked several times their weight in Japs just because Halsey told them they could, that's what it amounted to. He had a knack of making people do it.

Q: Would he come around, be in evidence often - did people get to see him?

van Deurs: Yes. He was out in the front of the thing. He went up to the front of the thing frequently, they'd see him, and he talked to people of all ranks, all grades. And he had, as I say, the gift of a wisecrack or a few words that were just the proper thing for the moment.

I wasn't there, some of my friends were --- the story of the early days of Guadalcanal, when they were still fighting, and the Japs were trying to retake Henderson Field. They had one end of the field, and Halsey insisted on going up there to try to improve morale. He thought it was his place. His staff tried to stop him, said, "No, you can't go in there, they're shooting right down the field."

"Well," he said, "a plane can come in and land over the Japs, go down to the end of the field, I can jump out and dive in a foxhole, and the plane can turn around and take-off again and get away with it." That's what he did.

This plane came in, landed, and he jumped out of the plane at the end of the runway and dove into a hole, with the Japs shooting down the runway at the plane. Then the pilot turned around and took-off the other way and got away with it.

Q: He had a lot of personal courage, no question of that.

van Deurs: Oh, no doubt about that.

He went all around with the commanding general that was there, a Marine General, and went through the front lines and so on with him, doing morale a lot of good.

The General had his own camp alongside the Lunga River. There was a high bluff, then some flat land near the river, and anything the Japs shot in that direction would go over the camp on account of the bluff. So the General took him down there and served him dinner. I guess Halsey didn't realize that an aide had spent a lot of time visiting a lot of ships that were out lying off, getting something to make the dinner with, but they ended up with a very good apple pie.

Halsey said - by golly, he had to see the cook that could make a pie like that under these conditions. The General said it wasn't necessary. No, he insisted he had to congratulate the cook.

He went around behind the tent, found a field kitchen with an old sergeant in torn pants, no shirt, and a dirty rag around his waist. He was the cook. Halsey laid it on pretty thick, I'm told, told him he was the kind of guy that made victory possible and so on. The Old Sergeant got more and more embarrassed, twisting this rag. He'd never seen so many stars in his life. Halsey kept pouring on the oil. Finally the guy had to say something, "Oh, horseshit, Admiral, 'twarn't nothin'." The story went all over the South Pacific.

A few months later Halsey was having lunch at our mess, said some thing was pretty good. "Admiral, would you like to congratulate the cook?" Moebus asked.

Halsey said, "It's a God damned lie, and furthermore I wasn't there."

It was things like that that made everybody like the guy, and do things for him.

Q: Sure, he had the human touch without question.

van Deurs: A bunch of us were standing on Henderson Field one day watching him take-off to go back to Noumea, and somebody said, "There goes a great guy." Everybody agreed with that.

So they said, "Did it ever hit you that people like Lee and Grant, and maybe Napoleon, had staffs that thought the same thing? They were live flesh and blood people as long as some of those people were alive to remember them." "When we're all dead, Halsey will just be a name in the history books, that's all, just a bunch of statistics."

That crack was one of the things that started me trying to write aviation books, the early history afterwards, because people like Bellinger and Towers and the other early birds, were dying off, without leaving any biographies or any human touch to be remembered by.

Q: I think the Insitute is doing it for exactly the same reason.

van Deurs: I think that's the big thing about this Oral History thing; it can keep records of some of those things.

Q: And make them real.

van Deurs: Yes, make them sort of like real people instead of ...

Admiral Halsey's story that was ghosted by some joker is a rather poor biography. It tells what he did, but doesn't tell much about Halsey.

Q: What did you say about being too modest?

van Deurs: A man writing his own biography is apt to be too modest, or leave out the personal touches of the thing.

Q: I hope not. I hope that's what the purpose of this Oral History is, so that you won't leave out items about yourself.

van Deurs: It's easier to tell stories on Halsey than to think of stories that might be worthwhile on myself. Halsey or anybody else that was being ghosted, it would be the same thing.

There's a biography of Spruance over there by Forrestal that is a tremendous disappointment. You can read the thing. It's a good history of the war, and Forrestal served on his staff for a big part of the war, but the man Spruance doesn't come through at all.

Q: He was a great man.

van Deurs: He was a great man, a very quiet man, with a great, great brain, but you'd never get it out of that book. He also was a very human man.

I don't know anything else right now that's worth talking about down there.

Q: Did you have any other contacts with Nimitz?

van Deurs: No, I never had very many contacts with Nimitz. A few right at the end of the war was all.

Mick Carney was a frequent contact down there. I told you I had to go down to Noumea frequently to straighten things out. I used to work with the planning group when I went down there that was headed up by an Irish brigadier, Marine. He later was in Palestine on a peace mission for the U. N. When the working day was over, I was very apt to get caught with Mick Carney and this Marine and do a little drinking. They were a couple of crazy Irishmen that could pour drinks into you till two o'clock in the morning, then at six they were up and ready to fight the war again, fresh as daisies. So after a couple of nights of playing with them I was always very glad to get in an airplane and fly back to Guadalcanal where there was nothing but a little shooting going on - it was much healthier. They were hard people to keep up with, also very smart people.

Q: I've never understood how a person can do that.

van Deurs: I don't know, maybe it was the Irish temperament in both of them.

Carney of course stayed with Halsey all through the war, and was later CNO. He was an extremely likeable friendly guy, and extremely sharp. He used to call himself not the Chief of Staff, but "the Head of the Dirty Tricks Department." He was responsible for thinking up a lot of tricks that we pulled off on the Japs. Carney was a good friend. I can't think of the Marine's name at the moment.

I haven't seen him since, but I've seen Carney on a lot of occasions.

Q: I think you gave a good picture of the activities in that part of the Solomons.

van Deurs: When the thing finally folded up, we came home on Swede's carrier. It was diverted from San Diego, came into San Francisco, dumped us off at Alameda. I found orders for two weeks leave, and then to go West and take command of CHENANGO. I also found a message from the Detail Officer in Washington to call him as soon as we got in. I got on the phone - "We were all thinking about two weeks leave, but how about getting along immediately? We want to get the fellow you're relieving back to the Solomons to take command of a patrol wing. It's got to move out of there."

"When you see him, you can tell him he'll be a commodore when he gets down there."

Q: You will be?

van Deurs: No, the man I'm relieving.

I said, "Gee, I've been out of the country for a year and a half. I don't want to give up the leave. I want a couple of weeks before I start. The hell with you."

Also I happened to know what that outfit was doing down there in the Solomons, and there wasn't any big hurry about getting a man down there to take over.

So they finally agreed I could have the two weeks leave. Ann had just moved out to San Francisco and had an apartment on Sutter Street, so we enjoyed that couple of weeks.

Then I went down to the district headquarters, showed them the orders, said, "How do I get going?"

"We don't know where the CHENANGO is, we'll have to ask Pearl Harbor." So they sent a dispatch. "Come back tomorrow."

I went back tomorrow. They didn't have anything. Next day they called up and said they had orders for me. "What are they?" "We can't tell you over the telephone." So I trotted down to the Federal Building. "Here's a dispatch from Pearl Harbor. It says, 'Direct Captain van Deurs to carry out his orders.'" Secret! - Bah, they couldn't put it over the telephone.

"That's fine, where do I go?" They had no idea. We'll send you to Pearl. I think it took them three more days. I said, "I'm enjoying San Francisco, having a swell time, I just happen to have had a phone call from Washington. They were kind of anxious to get me out there in a hurry."

It took them three more days to find an airplane seat for me. I enjoyed the delay very much; I was having fun. But when I did go, I went awful fast. I think I got into Pearl about eight in the morning, still not knowing where the ship was, went out to Nimitz's headquarters, found somebody who said, "Oh, it's in Kwajalein right now, but we don't know how long it's going to be there. It's about to leave there for the Admiralties, maybe you can catch it at Kwajalein and maybe you can't."

So I had about two hours in Pearl Harbor and got in another airplane and about midnight I was in Kwajalein. - tremendous lagoon full of ships. I finally found a base duty officer who had no idea where the CHENANGO was. I doubt they'd ever heard of her. They put me in a boat in the middle of the night to start down this lagoon trying to find it. I think about two in the morning maybe we found her, maybe twenty miles down the lagoon. The man I relieved was very glad to see me, Dixie Ketcham, a class ahead of me at the Naval Academy, and a very nice guy that I believe is still living down the Peninsula very quietly with his wife.

The easiest way for him to get to the Solomons and pick up his group was to go to the Admiralties and fly over from there. By that time they were connected up with the South Pacific. The next morning I went over to see Admiral Tommy Sprague, who was the division commander, and told Tommy I didn't think it was quite right - he didn't like the idea of a makee-learn captain being aboard. He thought when the new captain came aboard the old one ought to leave right now. But I finally convinced him I didn't mind and it was easier for Dixie, so Dixie kept the ship until we got down to the Admiralties. I think we sailed that afternoon and I took over there.

I was rather glad to see how somebody else ran it, because the last time I'd been on a ship I was a Lieutenant on the SARATOGA, and this thing was headed for Jap country, and I was just hoping I could measure up to it.

Q: That was an exciting assignment, wasn't it, to be the commanding officer?

van Deurs: I got to really love that ship. There were four of them that had been converted from tankers, and we had the same fighters that the big carriers did. The Kaiser Jeeps that were smaller couldn't carry them. They had to have smaller planes.

Q: How many planes did you carry?

van Derus: I think it was about thirty-eight. They were fighters and torpedo planes.

Q: No dive bombers, torpedo planes and fighters.

van Deurs: Yes, I think that was all they had. The fighters, of course, the FGF, were perfectly good dive bombers. They could carry a tremendous load. I used to watch them go off. We'd shoot them off taking I think around nineteen thousand pounds, and I used to kind of marvel at it, thinking back to the Ford Trimotor that we thought was an awfully big plane - carried twelve people and I think it was about twelve thousand fully loaded with three engines in it. These Hellcats with half as much again, with one engine, and one man - they were beautiful airplanes.

Q: How many officers and men?

van Deurs: Oh, I guess there were about two thousand or twenty-five hundred people on board. I've forgotten exactly.

There was one other interesting angle. She'd been out there for about a year; giving air cover for all the landings. She was down in the South Pacific when I was there, then used at Tarawa and all the landings from there on. The executive officer was the only other regular officer in the ship. When I took over I asked him if they had any particular problems and he said - the only thing was all these guys think they're specialists. "If somebody gets sick and I tell somebody to do his job for him he says, 'Oh, I haven't been to that school, I don't know.'" He said they could do it all right, they'd been out there long enough so everybody knows how to do pretty near anything, but they don't believe it.

I don't like to make speeches, but I sort of figured that people ought to have a chance to look at a new skipper and get some idea what his ideas were, so I got them together back in the wardroom, gave them a few of my ideas how to run the ship. I particularly mentioned that I thought a couple of years experience in the war zone was at least equal to four years sitting by the Severn and reading books about war, and if there was anybody on the ship that couldn't do any job that was there, I'd figure he was either awfully stupid or too damn lazy to do anything except stay in his bunk. I thought they were all professionals by this time.

Nobody ever pulled - "I didn't go to that school," on the exec again. They all got the idea. It was as swell a bunch as I ever went to sea with.

Dixie had trained about six or eight of them to stand the officer of the deck watches. He said his policy had been that they ran the ship whether he was on the bridge or not. He did spend a lot of time on the bridge. He said he never interfered unless someone made a serious mistake. They had orders to ignore the captain.

Well, gee, in the old Navy system before the war, you asked permission to change course two degrees and maybe the captain did it himself. In the middle of the night if you had to change course, why, you called the captain and he came on the bridge while you did it, and so on and so forth. None of the old captains lasted long after Pearl Harbor - they all had nervous breakdowns.

Dixie said he figured if he could be up there all day and see these kids doing everything right, why, they'd probably do it when he was catching some sleep at night. It seemed like a good system, and I followed it with the same kids. I think I got a full night's sleep practically every night, no matter where we were or how close we were to the shooting. They did a wonderful job on it.

I used to wonder what they'd do after the war, after being salted that way. I never found out. One of them was a biochemist, believe it or not, and spent some of his Navy pay to buy an interest in a drugstore, and he was perfectly convinced that he was going back to be a druggist when he got through. Yet he was the fire control officer of the ship and knew more about the fire control radars and stuff than anybody else.

Q: Did you have a CIC in your ship?

van Deurs: We had a CIC, yes.

The chemist was a number one watch stander. I somehow could never picture him going back to peeking through a microscope and putting prescriptions together.

One of them had been a chief signalman before the war. He was old Navy stuff, never worried about him, he did as good as any of them. He probably finished his thirty years and retired.

All the kids had the idea that after three or four or five years of this business they could go back to the home town and everything would be just the same as it was before.

Q: You can't ever go back.

van Deurs: You can't ever go back, but none of them realized it.

We had a little ensign, bomb disposal officer, every once in a while a plane would come back with a bomb hung up on the landing gear or one that didn't drop out of the bombbay or something, and when she hit the arresting gear the bomb would go shooting up the deck with the little propeller on the nose spinning to arm the fuse. The deck crew would dive for the safety nets and yell for this little ensign. He'd run dashing out on the deck, sit on the darned thing, pull out a pair of pliers or something, yank the fuse out of it, and throw it over the side, and then things would go on as normal. He thought he had the swellest job on the ship. Gee, he loved it. Nobody else would take it.

He was the only one I've ever seen since. I ran into him on Market Street one day and asked him what he was doing, shortly after I came here. He was working for the Golden State Dairy milk outfit. Somehow I couldn't figure him for the temperament to be a milk salesman. After thinking about it for a week I called up Golden State and tried to find him, but apparently he'd quit and disappeared. I don't know what happened to him.

CHENANGO was quite a ship; she would carry enough oil. They'd cut down the oil tanks originally and put berthing space and storerooms on top of them, but she still carried several million gallons of fuel oil, so that we could go for a month on an operation and fuel the destroyers that were with us all the time and never need oil ourselves.

The first operation I went over to Moratai, covered the landings there when we seized that.

Q: Before you do that, can you describe to me what position your carrier was and the surrounding ships and how many were in it?

van Deurs: On that operation we operated the four carriers of that type together as a division, and it was what we called a circular formation, although it looked like the carriers were forming a square. Around them was a screen of - I don't think we had any cruisers with us that time - destroyers with a lot of anti-aircraft guns. Things were spaced so that, the range of a forty mm gun was about four thousand yards, so the ships were spaced about four thousand yards apart. A plane coming in, everybody could shoot at them without worrying much about hitting the opposite ship.

Q: What were the other carriers?

van Deurs: The SAGAMMON, the SWANEE, the SANTEE. All four of them had been Standard Oil tankers before the war. They were twin screw, made about nineteen knots.

Q: Who was in charge? You said four carriers and destroyers and you were covering the landings on Moratai.

van Deurs: We covered the landings on Moratai.

Q: Where were the transports for the troops?

van Deurs: Going out there the transports were in a big convoy that was also surrounded by some cruisers and stuff.

Q: Separate cruisers?

van Deurs: They were usually operated separately from the carriers because cruising's their objective. We had to put up planes for anti-submarine patrol around the convoy all the time, so the carriers had to be free to maneuver to launch and land planes during the day.

Q: Did they follow you or were they ahead of you?

van Deurs: It depended on how the wind was. We stayed near them, let's put it that way. Tried to keep clear enough so that we could go in any direction we had to to handle planes.

Q: Were you in command of this operation?

van Deurs: No, the division commander, Tommy Sprugue. The SAGAMMON was his flagship, and he was in command of the carrier part. I think Admiral Wilkinson was running the amphibious end.

Q: And you were part then of the Seventh Fleet, when you were down in that area?

van Deurs: We were loaned to the Seventh Fleet for that operation. And that one was fairly quiet, a routine thing. You kept an antisubmarine patrol, and before the landing did a lot of bombing and strafing to soften up the beaches, but there wasn't any real air operation, I reckon. I don't think so. The Japanese air had either pulled out of that part of the world or there wasn't much of it. Moratai was very close to Halmahera. It's a much bigger island, and it had several landing fields, Japanese fields, so just as a routine measure we punched holes in those every morning to keep the Japs from using them to stage in planes to object to the landing.

Q: This was in support of MacArthur's march up New Guinea.

van Deurs: Towards the Philippines.

Q: The Seventh Fleet was under MacArthur at that time, wasn't it?

van Deurs: Oh, yes. Admiral Kinkaid was MacArthur's naval commander.

Halmahera was a big island that had a tremendous lagoon in the middle of it that was connected with the sea by a long narrow passage a couple of miles long, and there were a lot more Japs on Halmahera than there were on Moratai. Working over the fields there to keep them from using them, a plane got shot down one morning by ground fire. The pilot parachuted and landed in this, the inner end of this passage way to the lagoon. And there was a Japanese launch anchored off the beach there, nobody in it apparently, and he managed to get behind that and hang onto it, with a bunch of Japs shooting at him from the beach with machine guns, a little pier sticking out there. The group commander from my ship was leading the fighters that morning. He led the other fighters circling and diving on the Japs that were shooting at our man in the water and got on the radio and yelled for help. Sprague immediately sent another flight of fighters in to relieve them before they ran out of gas, and they kept it up for hours there, keeping anybody from bothering this man. He was in a life jacket in the water out there, just a hundred feet or so from the Japs on the beach, but the planes kept them too busy. Then the problem was - how to get him out of there?

They yelled for a Dumbo, as we used to call them, a Catalina rescue plane, seaplane, and sent him in there with heavy fighter escort that strafed everything around there, but there wasn't room for the Catalina to land and get to this man, so they came back.

They had brought some PT boats up to Moratai. In the meantime every hour or so we launched a new bunch of fighters to go in there and take over protecting the man.

Q: All this for one man.

van Deurs: Daylight flight was when he got shot down.

Q: I say, all of it for one man.

van Deurs: Yes. Then Sprague yelled, asked for a PT boat to go in there. It took a couple of hours to get it down from Moratai. Then this PT boat went in the narrow passageway, which was fortified on both sides. All the fighters that we could muster, loaded with bombs, rockets, machine guns, everything, strafing everything on both sides of it so no Jap could shoot at him. The PT boat went in, fished the guy out under the Jap guns, turned around and came out again.

Q: Isn't that incredible.

van Deurs: I think we lost one more plane and pilot during the day, covering him.

Q: Getting him.

van Deurs: Yes. But it did the pilot morale no end of good, because the word was out that Tommy Sprague would get 'em, would not abandon them.

Q: It was more really then than just the idea of getting one man.

van Deurs: It was the idea that you weren't going to write him off if you could possibly avoid it.

From then on the air group morale was pretty darned good, except they'd been out there too long. They were supposed to be relieved about six months. At that time they'd all been fighting for a year. Every time they thought they were going to be relieved the air group that was supposed to relieve them didn't get there. The ship got turned around to go for a new operation, go to Kwajalein then on to Moratai.

In the Admiralties while we were waiting there they wanted to put the air groups ashore on one of the airfields there and let them have some beer and so on and relax a little bit, and my Air Group Commander objected very strenuously - didn't want to go ashore, didn't want to take his people over there.

I said, "Why?" He said, "The fliers on some of these other ships are getting war fatigue, getting kind of low-spirited. My gang is in good shape. I don't want them to go over there and catch the disease." He objected strenuously - chap named Tom Moore.

One of the best fighter pilots I ever saw and a real natural leader - he kept that air group on their toes. He had to take them ashore though - Tommy Sprague insisted. But he brought them back still in good shape, wouldn't let them associate with the other people.

He had a broken nose that was pushed over to one side and very protruding big ears. Came up on the bridge laughing one day. He had been sitting back in the wardroom censoring the crew's mail and he came across a letter that described him as "the ugliest man in the Navy." He thought it was funny as hell. He was a great flier, a great leader.

Q: Moratai was what date, do you recall?

van Deurs: It was late summer of '44, maybe September — must have been about then. It was about the time we finished that Halsey's gang raided Formosa and the Philippines. They splashed so many Jap planes, and the last few days had such little resistance, that Halsey recommended that we change the whole scheme of the war.

The plan up to that time was to use Moratai as an air base, to cover MacArthur's landing on the south end of the Philippines, down at Mindinao, then he would gradually work up through the islands.

Halsey suggested that the whole schedule be stepped up. He said that if we attacked the Philippines immediately that the resistance would be low because they'd cleaned out all the Japanese air that they could find and sunk a lot of shipping and pretty well wrecked the place. And he recommended that they go immediately to Leyte Gulf. Nimitz agreed and MacArthur and the Joint Chiefs of Staff gave in, so instead of going along with piddling island-hopping operations we went back to the Admiralties, after Moratai, refueled and got ammunition. Very hurriedly they put together the plan for the landings for Leyte Gulf.

We sailed from the Admiralties, covering a convoy of Mac Arthur's troops, up to Leyte landing. Other troops joined up there. It was a case of speed up — as quick as we could get back there and get the troops loaded and go on to Leyte.

Q: Could you describe where the CHENANGO fitted into the task group, the task force?

van Deurs: That was the same thing, except for that landing they brought in a lot more carriers. They brought in fourteen Kaiser carriers. We operated with six carriers in a group, split up some of the division so that there were two Kaiser carriers working with us, and two other groups of six Kaiser carriers each. We got sea room and airplane room. I think the other carriers came from the Central Pacific. They were not at Moratai with us. We picked some of them up at the Admiralties. The bunch of us that were down in the Admiralties covered one of the convoys that went up to Leyte.

Leyte Gulf was a pretty big place, and the landings were inside of the Gulf. There wasn't room for the carriers to operate inside. We stayed outside off Samar, and kept the three groups separated, I don't know, maybe twenty miles, so that each had sea room for launching planes. The planes went in and covered the landing.

Q: What was your part?

van Deurs: I guess we still belonged to the Seventh Fleet. Yes, Halsey was entirely separate - he was down there.

Q: Oh, you were still part of the Seventh Fleet.

van Deurs: We were operating as part of the Seventh Fleet. The fast carriers and the fast battleships were operating separately under Nimitz. Part of that crossup that everybody made much of was a lot of misunderstanding. MacArthur was so damned insistent on having his own fleet and his own people that he wouldn't let, would not have any direct channel of communication between Halsey and the Seventh Fleet. There were no radio channels set up. Halsey was working for Nimitz, and so MacArthur wouldn't include him in any of the operations plans. They had this long complicated communications plan for the Seventh Fleet, that included us and all the amphibious things and so on, but there was no setup for that outfit to communicate directly with Halsey.

Q: That's hard to believe now, looking back.

van Deurs: No, it was part of MacArthur's hatred of the Navy or craving for power or something - I don't know which, but he insisted on it being that way.

So that the only way that a message could get from Kinkaid or MacArthur to Halsey was, it was encoded, sent in code to a radio station back in the Admiralties, and then re-transmitted there on what we called a Fox schedule, which was a broadcast to the Fleet that every ship copied, and they'd pick out messages that had their call signs on it and break the code. Everything was coded and when an operation was going on everything was graded "urgent" and no other messages ever got through. Operators never knew what was what, so the poor guys would have a big stack of messages and they'd just peel them off in the order they came and keep sending them out on the air. So it took hours for a message to get from Halsey to Kinkaid or vice versa.

Now, probably every ship did what we did on the CHENANGO. We put spare operators on spare equipment and fiddled around and found one of Halsey's frequencies and listened in. We were breaking some of the messages just to see what was going on.

Q: From the Admiralty to him?

van Deurs: No, what Halsey was saying, trying to tell what was going on with the fast carriers, working just a few miles from us.

Q: Oh, you tried to listen in on Halsey's frequency.

van Deurs: Yes. It was illegal, so to speak, but everybody was doing it, just trying to find out what was going on.

Q: You had to find out some way.

van Deurs: Yes. This thing went on for, I don't know two or three days I guess, more or less routine, sending planes in to support the troops on the beach, give them close support, also sending plane beyond them to bomb fields on Cebu and other islands around there that we could reach, to keep the Japanese from using them.

It started out as routine. Then we got word from a lot of sources that the Japanese were coming after us, and the Jap Fleet was coming out with their Sho Plan. A bunch of their battleships started off from Singapore. They took oil at Borneo, I think.

The submarines got into one of the outfits over by Palau on the far side of the Philippines. Submarines were trailing them long before they came within air range. Two or three days these people were coming. We didn't know exactly which way of course, and some more came out of Manila.

As it shaped up, as soon as they got within air range we had air surveillance on them too, and there was no element of surprise in it. We knew the big outfit was heading for San Bernardino Strait and the smaller outfit was heading for Surigao Strait down south.

Kinkaid sent Admiral Oldendorf down south with the old battleships that had been supporting the landing, to stop that outfit at Surigao Strait.

Q: Was Oldendorf also with the Seventh Fleet?

van Deurs: Yes, he was commanding the bombardment ships for the landing.

Q: I was just shown Admiral van Deurs chart showing the breakdown of the two fleets, and he points out that between the two of them there was actually no direct communication.

van Deurs: That is correct.

The main Japanese body at San Bernardino Strait - Halsey got two or three carrier groups in there, on the east side of the Philippines, that flew across and beat them up pretty badly, all one day there.

Now, Ted Sherman's group was closest, as I remember it, and probably the last to leave the outfit that evening.

Sherman had one habit that I've never seen written up, but I know when he was working down in the South Pacific, two or three times he was questioned as to whether he'd really sunk all the ships that he claimed he had at the time. A couple of times it proved out later that he had not. But Sherman said his policy was to claim everything and let somebody prove he was wrong.

I kind of think he did that the day he was working at San Bernardino. They did leave the Japs with a big eighteen-inch-gun battleship sinking, and the whole outfit was milling around, and it looked like it was headed back towards Manila. They thought they had quit.

In the meantime Sherman lost the PRINCETON because a bunch of planes appeared, apparently carrier planes coming from seaward, hit his carrier group, and went on and landed in the Philippines. We didn't know where they went.

Anyway, I suspect that the reports from pilots and Sherman and the other two task groups commanders were somewhat exaggerated, claiming more damage on the Japs than actually happened. As far as Halsey knew they were a defeated outfit that had turned tail and would be out of range in the morning.

During the day he sent one of the messages that started all the dispute, which as I remember read, "When directed by me, Task Group 38," which was all the battleships he had with him and some cruisers, "to guard San Bernardino Strait." But the thing read, "When directed by me."

Q: To whom did he send that message?

van Deurs: He sent that message to his own task force.

It was one of the messages that I read, that we broke on the ship, and apparently Kinkaid also broke it and read it direct. But Halsey never directed forming TF38. There's been a lot of argument about why and why not. There've been a lot of people, like Jock Clark and so on, who didn't have the responsibility that Halsey had at the moment, who second guessed the thing. But personally I suspect that he was very much influenced by the damage reports in from the pilots, and from the admirals that were under him.

Q: Thinking that the Japanese had been so badly damaged, he didn't feel it was necessary to do it.

van Deurs: Also he had his basic orders, that he was to cover MacArthur's landing, but if the Japanese Fleet appeared that was to be his primary objective.

Q: To destroy it.

van Deurs: And from the attack on the PRINCETON it looked like there was a flock of carriers coming down from Japan. We knew the carriers had mostly been in Japan. Afterwards we knew they were decoys, but there was no way for him to know at the time. They were decoys - they were carriers with half trained air groups, the boys didn't know how to land aboard. They launched them, they attacked the PRINCETON, then they went on to Filipino fields, so that - the decoys had no planes at all, no punch. That all came out afterwards.

A lot of the people were critics of Halsey. But there was supposed to be a patrol plane from Kinkaid's outfit go out and watch San Bernardino Strait that night. Something happened. There was an accident and the plane never got off, and nobody got the word back to Kinkaid that it hadn't gotten off. There was a lot of confusion at Leyte Gulf, I guess.

Oldendorf licked the outfit down in the south, that was all right.

Q: The Battle of Surigao Striat.

van Deurs: At Surigao, yes.

But the next morning the small carrier planes were all being launched to go in and do the routine chores for our outfit, cover the troops, and some were sent to chase everybody who got away from Oldendorf the night before, if they were still within range, to get them - just a routine dawn launch.

And in the middle of it, one of the pilots who had just taken off called back to Ziggy Sprague's flagship and said, "There are a lot of battleships up here with pagoda masts."

Sprague couldn't believe it, asked for a repeat, what was he talking about. He said afterwards, he realized he was surprised, but that was it. He started running and passed the word to all the other jeep carriers. They called their planes back to attack the Jap battleships. The Battle of Leyte Gulf has been well written up from that point on.

Q: Where were you?

van Deurs: I was a hundred miles away; I missed it. A couple of days before we lost a lot of planes in routine work, and Sprague sent me and one other carrier down to Moratai to get spare planes. They flew them in from the Solomons. We went down there, our pilot landed a bunch of cripples on the beach, flew out with new planes. We had given all our good planes to the other ships before we left, filled them up. We were on our way back when this thing broke loose We didn't get back until the fight was all over.

I was always mad about it, because originally among other ammunition we all had some armor piercing bombs aboard. Some time before they'd taken them out of all the ships, but I'd refused to give mine up. I was the only one that had armor piercing bombs, and I wanted a chance to use them. But there wasn't any target by the time we got back within range.

Q: That would have been late October. I'm reading now that you received two gold stars in lieu of the second and third Legion of Merit, and this refers to "for exceptional meritorious conduct in the performance of outstanding services as commanding officer of escort carrier division during combat operations agatinst Japanese, October 18-24 and October 28-29." Wouldn't that have been - those are the dates.

van Deurs: That was Leyte Gulf, yes, but the big fight was one day between the 24th and 28th.

Q: Those are the dates of Leyte Gulf.

van Deurs: Yes.

Q: And it says you were commanding officer of an escort carrier division.

van Deurs: Yes, escort carrier, not division.

Q: I was wondering about that.

van Deurs: No, that's wrong. Tommy Sprague hung that medal on me after we got back to Seattle.

The only thing that happened besides those battleships breaking through and shooting up the carriers -- I guess they sank one of them, the ST. LO, I believe, and later that same day the first kamikazes broke loose. They were looking particularly for the CHENANGO, which had distinctive markings. Instead of grey she had camouflage, zigzag painting on her. Tokyo Rose used to mention us frequently by name. Yeah, they were out to get the CHENANGO.

The Kamikazes came out, seems to me they sank one Kaiser. They hit the other three ships of the division I belonged to just before I joined up - the SAGAMMON, SANTEE, and SWANEE all took hits from Kamikazes, and they all survived.

A few days later the division was ordered back to the States for battle repairs. We came home by way of Pearl Harbor.

The ship that was sunk in the running fight early in the morning got most of her people off in life jackets. The officers managed to keep them together pretty well, but there was a lot of confusion in navigation and so nobody was quite sure exactly where she went down. It took about two days for planes to find them. Then we got most of the people. They'd been in the water for about two days.

Q: The JOHNSON was lost.

van Deurs: The JOHNSON was a destroyer, the only destroyer in the escort group. The others were DEs. The skipper of the JOHNSON pulled a terrific job of making a smokescreen. He just headed for the Jap Fleet firing his guns and torpedoes, and they blew him out of the water.

Q: Admiral Sprague certianly was credited with doing a wonderful job.

van Deurs: Yes, Ziggy did a wonderful job of getting out of there after he was caught, also all three groups were fighting back.

I don't know - the Japs were confused. If you read Admiral Ofstie's bombing survey after the war, he queried the Jap admiral very much about that thing, about why he turned away and so on. His answers never quite made sense to me.

Q: Why he didn't go ahead and ...

van Deurs: Yes, he insisted that he thought he had run into the carriers.

What happened - Ziggy was turning inside and he was turning way outside, so his much faster battleships never caught the nineteen knot carriers. People kept firing torpedoes at him from both DEs, and also planes were bombing and strafing, and when some ran out of ammunition they kept diving on his ships - that all busted up his formation. Ships were moving in all directions trying to avoid torpedoes and attacks. His whole force got disorganized. But why he pulled off and turned around, Lord knows.

Q: This was Kurita?

van Deurs: Yes, I think so.

Kinkaid, as soon as he heard what was happening, ordered Oldendorf to get out there, but Oldendorf had a couple of hundred miles to go. He started, but I found out afterwards they weren't very anxious to get there - they'd used up pretty nearly all their ammunition the night before. They weren't in any position to take on a fleet action.

Q: You say the ST. LO survivors were in the water for two days before they were picked up.

van Deurs: The exec, Dick Ballenger, told me a funny story afterwards. He said, along towards the end of the second day he was kind of blue, but the gang kept pretty well bunched together ...

Q: He was in the water?

van Deurs: He was in the water, and he said he was feeling pretty low, wasn't sure they were ever going to be found. Some kid seaman came paddling up to him and said, "Commander, they say we get thirty days leave when we get out of this. We're survivors."

He said, "That's been the custom. Survivors get thirty days leave in the States." The kid went swimming back, "Yes, that's right. The Commander says that's correct."

Dick said the kid wasn't worried at all, but Dick was pretty damned well worried about that time.

Q: So you came back to the States after that.

van Deurs: We came back for repairs. The other three skippers were relieved, but I managed to hold onto the ship and take her back out. Two of the division were in Bremerton, the FRANKLIN was in Bremerton. They took one of them, the SANTEE, down in southern California, but they had me in the shipyard in South Seattle.

They ordered a lot of alterations as well as repairs. We got a second catapult, I think, for one thing, and to make extra space they added a couple more staterooms under the flight deck up forward that stuck over the side like perfectly square boxes. I objected to them, squawked to the naval constructors until they put some fairing in there and faired it up so that the sea would't batter them every time we stuck our nose down. The other ships didn't get that fairing.

We were almost through with the repairs when the SARATOGA and a couple of other carriers got hit off Iwo Jima. A dispatch from the Department told the Navy Yard to knock off all work in the carriers, button them as quick as they could, and start them west. So we left individually as fast as we could get the holes in the bottom plugged up, grabbed some ammunition at Port Townsend, came dwon to San Francisco for a new air group, and headed west.

It was winter time, January, and I boiled out of Port Townsend with all the nineteen knots she'd do heading down the Coast. They told me that there'd be a blimp from Tilamook out to give me submarine coverage the next morning. We were bucking a south wind and the seas were lapping up to the flight deck, making me glad I had that fairing. Clouds down almost to the top of the mast - it was kind of nasty weather.

I didn't see any blimp for a long while. Finally somebody looked astern and there was a blimp about half a mile astern of us. The car was swinging about forty degrees on each side. He was having an awful time flying the thing. Poor guy, it was a kind of lousy submarine position, but this guy broke out a blinker light and he was sending us messages - he couldn't keep up, couldn't catch us. He tried for a couple of hours, finally sent one that he was going back to base.

The SAGAMON and SAWANEE out of Bremerton got away ahead of me. I was the third one out. I think I got down to the Farrillones first. It was too rough for the pilot boat to come alongside, so I went in the channel without a pilot. I'd done it a couple of times before.

Q: Came into San Francisco Bay?

van Deurs: Came into San Francisco, and picked up a docking pilot, and they put me down at Hunter's Point. Seas had knocked a gun out of position on the trip down through the seas. They put me in there for a day to repair that. The other two ships that were ahead of me steamed around in circles for two days before they could get a pilot and come in. By the time they got in I had the air group ready on board and was taking off.

At Hunter's Point there was another carrier - I've forgotten which one of the big carriers - across the dock for a lot of repairs. She'd been hit by a Kamikaze. The skipper was Joe Bolger.

I went over to see Joe and he told me about the Kamikaze attack they had. He was much impressed by one forty mm gunmount that was entirely manned by Negro mess boys. This Kamikaze dove at that mount. Joe said the gun kept shooting until the Kamikaze hit it - wiped out the gun crew and knocked the gun off the side, but not a one of them left his post. They were still shooting when they died. He was very much a convert to desegregation.

Q: The new development, the Kamikaze, started just after Leyte?

van Deurs: It started just at Leyte Gulf, just at that time. Before that there'd been times when a pilot that had apparently been injured or something decided to crash on board, but the deliberate action had started there at Leyte Gulf.

I had a new air group and they gave me a destroyer to go with me to Honolulu, so I could work the planes out a bit on the way. They weren't too well trained. I think they busted up about half the airplanes between San Francisco and Honolulu, trying to get 'em in shape.

Q: Were they new pilots?

van Derus: New pilots, new air group.

We had a new air officer, an Academy man who had leanred to fly a littlebit later than most of his class; he was very nervous. I kept hoping he'd steady down; he didn't. In flight operations

I found out I had to almost stand behind him and frequently grab his hand to keep him from poking the wrong button or the wrong signal. It was kind of a nervous business.

Got to Pearl, and were in there a couple of days. I think I told you, while I was there I went around and thanked somebody for having given me good service down in the South Pacific and found L. C. Stevenson had issued orders to - if they saw my name on a dispatch, do it quick and don't ask any question.

Q: What about the damaged planes?

van Deurs: They had spares at Pearl, at Ford Island we got replacements.

I guess I waited there for the SAGAMMON. Sprague had been relieved. Bill Sample was the Admiral, and the two of us were sent down to Guadalcanal from Pearl to cover a convoy of the First Marines leaving the Solomons for the Okinawa assault. The time table was pretty fast. We didn't have much time to do flying on the way down, could not lose time turning around, practically a direct run over, as I remember, except we did divert to look for wreckage. Lieutenant General Harmon, who had been Halsey's Army Commander down in the South Pacific, was lost in a plane about that time, somewhere flying across the Pacific, so we looked for him but we never found any trace of him.

We got to Guadalcanal just as the Marines were practicing the assault landing on Guadalcanal, getting ready for Okinawa. We got their operation order, the plan of it, by radio, and launched some planes before we got to port to do the support part of it. Then we were in Florida Harbor for two or three days while they reloaded the transports in Iron Bottom Bay.

Taking advantage of being down there, I got a boat and went over to Guadalcanal to see what our old camp looked like. This was February, I had left Guadalcanal in June. The island was a network of hard coral roads, looked like pavement, camps all over, big ammunition dumps - very much a going concern.

The camp we'd used was still in use. I spent the night there. For breakfast had papaya off of little papaya trees we'd planted while we were there. Just in that six months the jungle had come back and come right on through the coral roads. There were millions of bombs and artillery shells in the jungle that were completely overgrown. They had pulled out all the troops, and then sent ships down there to get some of that gear. But the general commanding the island had nobody to do the loading. So I don't know the jungle had just reclaimed practically everything that had been built in Guadalanal in that six months. I suppose the same thing had happened on all the other islands. It was amazing how quick it happened.

I went over with Sample to see Reifsnider, who was commanding the amphibious outfit. Went to see what instructione he had for the trip north. His were all new transports that had just been built. Most of the people on them had never gone to sea before, officers or men. Some of them had left Seattle while I was there - nice looking ships. But Reifsnider said they didn't know what was going to happen if they ever had to turn a corner; they were awful green. The usual instructions were just to operate nearby for anti-submarine protection, didn't want anything else. There were quite a few ships in the convoy, three or four columns of four or five ships each around there.

General Geiger was commanding the troops. Well, we'd known him. He was on the flagship. Decided to go and say good morning to him before I left. Found him in a stateroom, nothing on but a pair of drawers, lying on the bunk reading a detective story.

I said, "You don't seem very worried about this." "Oh," he said, "nothing to it. Reifsnider will put us ashore and then we'll lick 'em. In the meantime I don't have anything to do.".

We started out operating the carriers a few miles astern of this transport formation, following along, and turning out when we had to launch planes. The first thing that happened — somebody's steering gear went bad on a transport, and suddenly ships were turning in all directions. We were completely surrounded by ships going in fifteen different ways. After that Bill kept the carriers well out to one side. We never got behind them again.

Q: How many were in the group under Sample - how many carriers?

van Deurs: There were just two carriers, the SAGAMMON and the CHENANGO.

Q: The SAGAMMON, that was his flagship, and yours, two destroyers?

van Deurs: We had two or three destroyers with us, and there were some more destroyers screening the transports.

We made Ulithi finally and got inside and anchored. That was a tremendous activity at the time, thousands of ships in there. It was the closest place to Okinawa to repair ships, so they concentrated all the floating tenders, repair ships, and floating drydocks there. Convoys were gathering, we were just one of a dozen convoys. It's an enormous lagoon with very little dry land.

Scrappy Kessing was the base commander there. Scrappy was quite a chracter. He'd been a character all his life. I think he'd been passed over, or retired, and called back - I've forgotten - but he'd been down in the South Pacific in the early days. He contacted some kind of a funny tropical disease. They shipped him back to the States and he ended up in Bethesda. They finally cured him and he wanted orders to go back to the war, but they stalled on him. He walked over to Anacostia and thumbed a ride in an airplane. Using nothing but his thumb he got out there and walked into Halsey's office in Noumea a little bit later and said, "Boss, I'm back, gimme a job."

"Where are your orders?" "Oh, they've still got me on the books at Bethesda, but I'm all well."

About the time that they were begging us to take Chet Bates out of Bougainville, so, "Okay, go up to Bougainville, you're the base commander." He did.

When we took Subic Bay, he went in there and set up the naval base at Subic Bay. The Philippine government was going to take over the old Army-Navy Club property at Manila, which was pretty well shot up. Somebody told Scrappy about it. The last secretary had buried the records of the club, and Scrappy swore he had proxies from me and everybody else that ever belonged to the Army-Navy Club and managed to take over and hold the place.

By the time we got to Ulithi he was moved up there as the base commander. He was quite a character.

Q: I wonder if his records ever caught up with him?

van Deurs: I asked him about that. He said, "Oh yes, Bill Halsey fixed that up all right."

He was running the beach at Ulithi, and something of a practical joker. All through those islands to act as urinals they'd drive a piece of two inch pipe down into the coral and solder a funnel on top of it with a very fine mesh screen. That kept the flies out of it, and the ground absorbed the stuff and kept it sanitary.

Running a bunch of the repair ships out in the lagoon was a very short officer named John Tom Bottom. He stood about five feet tall. At Scrappy's camp over on the island they had one of these pipes driven down so it was just about a foot above the ground and a sign on it, "Reserved for Commodore Bottom."

He loved to do things like that in his spare time.

Q: It never occurred to me about the plumbing facilities down in those areas until you just mentioned this.

van Deurs: We put those things at convenient places all over coral islands. Although some of us got ritzy on Guadalcanal - we put in a water system with flush toilets, a little bit of luxury.

Q: On other islands what would you do for the rest of it?

van Deurs: Dig a trench.

Q: Cover it up every day?

van Deurs: Cover it up, chlorate of lime. When it got full we moved it.

There was a story on Guadalcanal that Halsey and McCain and Fitch were looking around the place just before Fitch relieved McCain, and a bombing raid came in. Everybody dove for foxholes, and McCain came up covered with the stuff. He'd dived into a hole where they'd just moved a latrine and hadn't had time to fill up the hole. But he stayed in it till the raid was over.

Q: Do you think it's true?

van Deurs: I think it's true. Fitch told me, and he always referred to McCain as his "redfaced classmate" after that.

Q: I'm sure nobody cared about putting up walls or any of those little nicities.

van Deurs: There wasn't any use. There were no females in the darned place. It was a man's world.

Q: I've never before heard a reference about it until you told the story, which I think was interesting.

van Deurs: That was just one of the practical arrangements.

In the South Pacific a message came down from one of the islands one day that they were completely out of toilet paper. It created quite a flap. We got a shipload going up there. It's funny, of course, till somebody says to you, "Can you imagine ten thousand men on a little island and no place to put it?" It was more serious than running out of chow really.

Q: Sure, I guess so.

van Deurs: At Ulithi they gathered most of the assault force for Okinawa, and all the fast carriers were in there, lined up in what we called "Murderers' Row."

We were lying there and the carrier FRANKLIN came in, after a Kamakazi had destroyed her air group on deck and started a bad fire. She'd been at Bremerton being overhauled the same time I was, got out of there the same time. The air officer, Bill Hale, had been in my squadron at Pearl Harbor, and just a couple of days before we sailed I'd talked to him on the dock where he was supervising, getting something aboard. I didn't find out till a lot later that he was one of the FRANKLIN survivors.

When they anchored in Ulithi, not far from us, we could see through the ship, the whole length of the thing, where she was burned out. The skipper, Les Gehres, had been the executive officer on Ford Island part of the time I was there. I always thought it was a shame after bringing his ship out the way he did, they should have promoted him. But Gehres often talked before he thought, usually talked loud. Instead of commending a lot of the people for their heroic work in saving his ship, I understood he sounded off with a lot of kicks, said he had a near mutiny, had to pull a gun to make people do the work, and that people were shirking and trying to abandon ship.

Q: I didn't know that.

van Deurs: It was all hushed up and the story I heard was probably very much exaggerated, but he never went any further.

Q: Because he did pull a gun? Do you think he did?

van Deurs: I don't know. I never heard all the details of the thing, but according to his report I understand everything was wrong and he had practically a mutiny on his hands trying to save the ship. The loss of life was so heavy that some people criticized him and said he should have abandoned. But I always thought if he'd played it smart he would have been an admiral instead of being retired as a captain. But that's the way things happen.

Q: What date did the force leave Ulithi to go to Okinawa?

van Deurs: I don't remember when we got out of there. The assault on Okinawa was April Fool's Day. The night before it happened, the ocean was full of ships, Army convoys from Ulithi by the dozen, also convoys from Guam and Saipan, and I believe some came right from Pearl. They all converged on Okinawa for the assault.

Q: What force were you part of in this operation?

van Deurs: We covered that convoy all the way up to Okinawa. We joined up with a couple of others, as I remember, that also had carriers with them, and when we got up there these small carriers were all stationed off the island to give the troops close support on the landing.

Q: The operations orders on that landing must have been inches and inches thick.

van Deurs: They were tremendously thick.
Funny, one thing that I'm not sure people know — when I got to the War College after the war they were using the operations orders for those amphibious landings as models. That was the way you did it. Kelly Turner wrote most of them, and operated most of them.
He was the amphibious commander on all the big landings. And Kelly Turner was a very unusual man. He was in the same flight clas

with Ernie King down at Pensacola. He was kind of a dour sort of a bird, very serious, flew for a couple of years and then got out of aviation to take command of a cruiser and so on. At the beginning of the war I believe he was in intelligence in Washington at the time the word did not get to Pearl Harbor. But he also commanded the amphibious landing at Guadalcanal and most landings from there on.

Turner learned quickly by mistakes. After Guadalcanal and Tarawa he demanded and got all kinds of new equipment and different equipment - new type landing craft and so on. After the trouble at Tarawa he again made improvements on the things. He had a mind that could keep track of a thousand details all at once.

So in his operations orders, all the information fed into his flagship and fed him personally. There were air support groups, there were rocket ships, there were bombardment ships, there were the landing crafts, the transports —he had all those things actually getting ready for the assault. It was all split second timing, and things would go foul, get fouled up one place or another. The foul-ups would be reported by voice radio to Kelly Turner on the bridge of his flagship. He would make a decision right there and give them an answer. He was the only man I know of that could keep track of all of these things going on at once, because he'd done an awful lot of the order writing in the first place and okayed all of it. He was completely familiar with it. But it took a million radio circuits all going to the bridge and the amphibious flagship.

Each operation after the first week maybe, when the troops were secure ashore and the general had moved his headquarters to the beach, the general took care of the fighting, called for what ship or air support he needed. After that stage was operating smoothly Turner would turn over to the next senior amphibious admiral. Turner would go back to Guam or Pearl to start working up the next operation.

And as soon as he left, things would fall apart because there was nobody that could keep track of details the way he did. Whoever was left to fill his shoes just couldn't do it. Nobody except Turner could keep track of all the details that were happening at once.

Q: I know he was a brilliant man.

van Deurs: He was a brilliant man. He was tough and he was peculiar and he had to do things his own way, but he could handle that kind of an operation where nobody else could.

Q: He was sure a needed man at the time.

van Deurs: There's probably some way to accomplish the same thing by delegating certain responsibilities and splitting the mental load at a time like that, but Turner never did it. His orders were never written that. They all worked. They worked well -- as long as he had his hand on the throttle and was making instant decisions on each foulup, but I don't know of anybody else that could do it.

The Japs never realized that if they'd ever made a hit on the amphibious flagship going in there and removed Kelly Turner, the operation would have probably fallen on its face. It just didn't happe so ...

Q: What was your position off Okinawa, your ship's position?

van Deurs: We were off Okinawa for three or four days giving troop support, flying missions in there. One plane from the CHENANGO was the first American plane that landed on Okinawa, after the assault. There was not any opposition at the beach and the troops ran right across the island, and then split, and one outfit went north and the other outfit went south. They overran Kadena airfield the first day. This plane of mine, torpedo plane, had some kind of trouble and flopped into Kadena airfield.

Q: Oh, not on purpose?

van Deurs: Not on purpose. It landed in there, and they had an awful time. They didn't have any mess kits with them and there was no way for the assault troops to get anything to eat unless you got in a chow line with a mess kit. They needed some gasoline, but no gasoline had been landed yet. They went around the place and everybody was too busy to give them the time of day or help them out at all.

Finally they found some gas drums that they thought had Japanese gasoline in them. They didn't know how good it was, but they put some in the tank and fixed up whatever forced them to land, did a patchup job - took them a couple of days. They finally got into the air with the machine and came home.

Q: Did you know where they were? Had they been able to communicate?

van Deurs: Some of the other planes told us. Their radio was out. Some of the other planes told us they saw them land on Kadena and they were all right, but we couldn't get communication with them and they couldn't with us.

About three days later, I remember, they joined up and came home following one of our groups. The engine complaining a bit, but still running on the Japanese gasoline. They landed and rolled up into the spot, and all three of the men jumped out and got on their knees and kissed the deck. They were awfully glad to get home.

Q: I bet they were. You use the words "came home." Did the men themselves feel that way about the ship, think of it as "home"?

van Deurs: Oh, yes, absolutely.

South of Okinawa there were a bunch of islands called Sakishima, the Sakishima group or Sakishima gunto. There were two or three airfields in them. The Japanese were getting hard up for airplanes, but they still had planes on Formosa that could cause trouble if they could refuel at Sakishima and then go on to Okinawa.

The British Fleet had come out by then with several big carriers and they were given the job of neutralizing those fields at Sakishima. They stayed there three or four days and then sent signals that they had to go back to Australia for overhaul and left. So the four carriers of my division were sent down there to replace the British Fleet and keep those fields inoperative.

Admiral Bill Sample, the division commander, I think ran up some sort of a record. He was there for eighty-one days without seeing land.

Q: That means all of you were?

van Deurs: No. He was the Admiral. The rest of us didn't have quite that much of a record, because we ran out of ammunition and had to go get ammunition one at a time.

Those four little carriers managed to keep a patrol over the Japanese airfields twenty-four hours a day. We bombed and strafed them every morning. If they had a plane hidden anywhere and tried to bring it out at night, and showed a light, something dropped on them. We were just flying over the place all the time.

The carriers ran out of ammunition or ran low on it. So at night one ship would leave the formation and steam by itself during the night and show up at the nets of Kerama Retto at first daylight. The Japanese were bombing Kerama Retto every night so we wouldn't let a carrier stay in there overnight. We'd just dash in at daylight, load ammunition all day as fast as we could - never get filled up - and leave about sunset, just before the Japanese were due, then steam around all night and join up with the formation the next morning.

When the flagship went in, Bill shifted over to one of the other ships, which is why he made the eighty-one or ninety-one day record, and the rest of us broke it a couple of times by going in for ammo.

Q: You were there in that area three months?

van Deurs: From April to June, I think. The fighting went on on Okinawa. The CHENANGO had her worst casualty there.

It took a pretty tight schedule to keep the place worked over. We didn't have too many planes. So we were running a schedule where they'd land planes and as quick as they were re-armed they'd go off again, and we took chances that we never would in peacetime. Before landing planes we had a lot of bombs and rockets on the flight deck ready for them. As soon as the plane rolled out of the arresting gear and parked up on the bow, men began reloading it and putting fuel in it, while the rest of the planes were landing. When a plane rolled in they were waiting for it.

About six planes were on the bow, as I remember it, and the gas and big bombs and lots of rockets up there. A plane came in, perfect landing - it turned out there was a soft plank in the deck. It was behind one of the metal cross pieces that you use to tie down. And the hook gouged into that soft wood, hit the metal, and snapped off. So instead of catching number one wire, this plane rolled along, bounced over all the barriers. It landed right on top of the planes in the bow that were being refueled, and exploded. We had quite a terrific fire. The rockets began going off and shooting right down the flight deck, so we had to clear the flight deck. Two or three carriers had had a hit or a fire on the bow and gotten badly damaged and lost a lot of people by turning the wrong way which wrapped the fire around the island and the bridge. I crossed my fingers and hope I was turning out of the wind the right way. I turned cross wind so the fire was blown off to port away from the bridge and away from the flight deck.

One destroyer followed us and the rest of the ships went on with the operation.

It took us five or six hours to put the fire out, and there was a lot of heroic stuff done - what with this ammunition going and gasoline being in the waterways. Some I saw from the bridge and some of which I just heard about afterwards, I didn't see it. People started fighting the fires from the nets on the side. There were people jumping up on planes that were already burning, yanking the ammunition out of the guns and throwing it over the side, people yanking bombs that were parked right in the middle of the fire and throwing them over the side. The top chief of the flight deck grabbed a tractor, backed it up to a plane on the windward side that wasn't quite burning yet, though its paint was blistered, man jumped out of the nets and hooked towbar onto the plane, and the chief towed it aft. I think he snagged two planes out of the fire that way that were just about to catch fire.

The first explosion had killed - I think I lost about thirteen men. It blew several over the side, and I never saw them go but the destroyer that followed us saw them go and stopped and picked them up.

The bow of the ship stuck out a little bit further than the flight deck. At the front of the flight deck were a couple of gun tubs that had twenty mm guns in them. The explosion had pushed a plane over into one of those gun tubs with a five hundred pound bomb underneath it. It was wedged on the deck. A couple of men stood in that gun tub for about three hours, playing a hose on that bomb to cool it, while other men further back played another hose on the men to keep them from catching fire, with fire all around them. Gasoline was running wild all over, burning waterways, dripping down and burning on the forecastle underneath the men cooling the bomb. They stayed there the whole damn time and kept that bomb from blowing the front end of the ship off.

Q: I don't know how they did it.

vanDeurs: It was fortunate, that while we were in Seattle I'd insisted that everybody go through the Navy Fire Fighting School. I wanted to do it myself, but I was the only one that never got to it. It paid off, because these kids knew exactly what to do with the equipment and were not afraid of the fire.

Q: Were they using foam?

van Deurs: They used some foam but mostly fine spray, like a fog, with a fog nozzle. That was what they were turning on these men to keep them cool.

Q: They didn't have any particular gear, did they?

van Deurs: No, they were in dungarees.

The front end of the ship got full of gasoline fumes. The first lieutenant came up and said he was afraid a spark would explode it down below. So we had the engineer pull the circuits, take all electricity off the front end of the ship. That killed all the radio, so we didn't have any radio or radar or CIC. They were all dead.

We finally got it out. The planes had melted. The aluminum had melted, run down and solidified in the catapult track, in the slot the cable ran in for the catapult, and there was a big hole in the front of the flight deck. About six or eight planes were shot. The other planes were in the air and had been able to land on some of the other carriers. That took care of them.

Q: Those two boys on the front lived through it?

van Deurs: They lived through it. The bomb didn't go off. They finally got to it and threw it overboard. They worked into the fire, grabbed it, and got it over the side. They got the fire out about sunset.

Q: Should I ask you - have you ever had a worse experience?

van Deurs: Oh, I don't know. That lasted a long time, it seemed, with ammunition flying around.

Q: Were you giving orders personally yourself?

van Deurs: No, fighting the fire was Elwin Farrington's, the exec's, job. I was on the bridge watching it, and a few times I saw something that he couldn't see from down on deck and used the megaphone to tell him about it, but that was all. All I could do was keep the ship headed the right way. The machine gun ammunition was going off. It was bouncing in all directions. The quartermaster or somebody came along and put a tin hat on me. I did send the helmsman down below to steer from the inside, to get him out of it. But it was just a long afternoon.

Q: To say the least!

van Deurs: By the time it was over the doctor came up and allowed that he had to get rid of the bodies right quick, they were in pretty bad shape, so we had a funeral that evening and buried them at sea.

Q: That must have been a terribly sad experience.

van Deurs: The people worked through the night in the dark without any lights, but they managed to clear the catapult track and patch the hole in the flight deck, so by daylight the next morning we were able to report ready for flight operations again.

Q: That's incredible.

van Deurs: I think that was where I got one Legion of Merit.

Q: Yes, you have a third Legion of Merit which I do want to read.

It says, "As commanding officer of the USS CHENANGO, during operations against enemy Japanese forces in the vicinity of Sakishima Gunto and Okinawa on April 9, 1945, when a landing plane started a raging fire on the flight deck, among parked planes loaded with bombs, rockets, and fifty calibre ammunition, Captain van Deurs assisted in averting disaster by expertly directing fire fighting and bomb disposal forces and contributed materially to restoring the CHENANGO to normal operations within a few hours, thereby enabling the ship to remain in action for an additional sixty-six days."

So this is essentially correct.

van Deurs: Yes.

It was funny — I saw things like that chief on the tractor, and I saw a whole flock of men do remarkably daring things, looking down from the bridge at it, but most of them I couldn't recognize. They were just guys in dungarees and an undershirt or something. I was looking down on them and didn't ever see the faces.

As soon as the fire was out, the exec came up on the bridge and said, "Gee is the smoking lamp lit up here? I sure need a cigarette." He'd been down in the middle of it all the time.

We tried to make a list right then of the people that had done something, and we got a few names down. I remembered the top chief. I said, "Who of the kids jumped out and put the towbar on that burning plane?" Gee, he didn't know; he hadn't seen 'em. He mentioned a couple of things, and told about these kids on the gun tubs. We finally found out who those were. But nobody would come forward and say he was the guy who did this or that. I mentioned two or three things that had happened right alongside of where Farrington was standing and he said, "Gee, I didn't see that happen, where was I?" "You were about five feet over here on the other side doing something else."

We got probably twenty or thirty names we nailed down, but there were probably three times as many that deserved a medal for it, and we never could find out. We spent a couple of days quizzing everybody on deck, officers and men, as to who the guy was that did this or who the guy was who did that. Nobody would admit doing any of it.

Q: Maybe under the pressure of the situation they could have done it and not even remembered. Is that possible?

van Deurs: I don't know. Some of it was pretty good stuff.

Everybody that we could find the name of we recommended for a medal, and they all got it, but there were a lot of them that deserved it that I never could find out what their names were.

Q: It says, "an additional sixty-six days."

van Deurs: Something like that. Same business, Sakishima.

Actually my relief was on board, I think, when the fire happened. I got a postcard from Moebus who had taken the SARATOGA home after she was battered. He'd been ordered to Washington. A destroyer came along with some mail one day at Sakishma, and a postcard from

Washington that said, "Brother, I see you're going right back where you started," signed "Brother." It didn't mean anything to me. I scratched my head over it for a couple of weeks, but it didn't mean anything.

Then another destroyer came along, said they had a passenger for us, sent him over on the trolley. It was Don Felt with orders to relieve me. (He later was Commander-in-Chief Pacific.) I said, "Well, that's nice, but I haven't got any orders to go anywhere. Sit down and have a cup of coffee and make yourself at home. I'm not turning over."

I sent a signal over to Bill Sample, told him my relief was there, but I didn't have any orders. So we steamed around for another week or so. In the meantime this fire happened.

Finally another mail came along with orders for me to go report to San Francisco for transportation to whatever port Admiral Oldendorf was in and report as Admiral Oldendorf's Chief of Staff. From the operation orders I knew Admiral Oldendorf was about fifty miles away at Okinawa, and I wasn't about to go back to San Francisco.

I thought about it. I could get some leave. But then agreed with Sample. The next time we went in for ammunition I'd give Felt the ship and then go from Kerama Retto to find Oldendorf. I was kind of sore about it. I was enjoying the ship. I loved it, liked the people in her, it was a lot of fun being skipper of a carrier.

Got into Kerama Retto, turned over to Don in the middle of a rainstorm, got into a whaleboat with my suitcase, went over to the SOPA and asked him how I could ride the twenty miles over to Okinawa. Nobody knew.

I saw a couple of battleships loading ammunition over in one corner and knew they were part of Oldendorf's bombardment outfit, so I sent an unofficial signal to the skipper of one of them and asked if he'd take me to Okinawa? Got an answer - yes.

So I got in the whaleboat and got in another rainstorm. I was soaking wet when I climbed the NEW MEXICO's sea ladder feeling like a wet stray dog. As I got to the top of the ladder, a lieutenant with more eagle guts on his shoulder than I'd seen in a long time gave me a very snappy salute, "The Chief of Staff wants to see you."

"That's fine, whose flagship is this, anyway?"

"Admiral Spruance's."

I hadn't realized that when I sent the signal. "Who's the Chief of Staff?"

The Chief of Staff was Art Davis, who'd been in my flight class at Pensacola. He was a very smart man and an old friend.

So I went down and told Art I was pretty sore, didn't know why I'd been snatched off a good carrier to go to a battleship when I hadn't been on one since I was an ensign and I didn't want any part of them. He calmed me down and explained what the job was.

And I said, "Furthermore I've never seen Oldendorf. I don't know what he looks like. I don't know why I was picked for his Chief of Staff. Why doesn't he pick somebody he knows?"

He proceeded to tell me a lot about Oldendorf that would come in handy later. He said, "By the way, have you met Admiral Spruance?"

I said, "I met him years ago casually. I've never known him. He wouldn't know me from Adam." "Well, come on, you've got to meet him."

Q: You were still soaking wet?

van Deurs: More or less.

I said, "No, don't bother the man."

Here's the man that was in charge of the whole battle, and they were still fighting like hell on Okinawa. The big shot that was running the show would have no time for me.

Art insisted, dragged me across the corridor to the Admiral's cabin. Spruance was sitting behind a desk that had nothing on it reading a book. I always suspected it was a novel, but I'm not sure.

Very gracious, asked me to sit down, tried to make a little small talk conversation. Spruance never had any cocktail conversation. He never could make small talk. He never wasted a word in his life. But he tried to be the genial host.

In the meantime Art ducked out, went back to work, and left me at the Old Man's mercy. Very soon the Old Man said, "Van Deurs, Van Deurs, didn't you take the War College correspondence course once?"

I said, "Yes, twenty years or so ago, why?"

"Well, I just happened to be running that correspondence course when you took it."

I said, "For crying out loud, what did I do that was so horrible that you remember my name at a time like this?"

"Oh," he said, "nothing at all, nothing at all - you finished the course, didn't you?"

I said, "Yes."

He said, "An awful lot of people used to start that thing in those days and then never finish it. I just made it a point to remember the names of people that finished it."

Well, that left me kind of breathless, for a bird that was running the biggest fight the Navy ever had, and he could bring up something like that out of the past. It was a kind of a brain I wasn't used to.

That night, I was a guest in his mess and ended up sitting on his left. A classmate of mine on the staff sat on the other side of me. The boy carefully put a percolator between me and the Admiral with the makings for some coffee. I'd heard that he was a coffee fiend.

When he and Nimitz were living together at Pearl Harbor, early in the war, we used to get a message down in the South Pacific once in a while, "Send up a sack of coffee beans." There were coffee beans on the plantations we'd taken over at Espiritu Santo. We'd shake a tree and throw a sack of coffee beans in the next plane north. We understood that the two admirals were roasting their own and blending it with some Kona coffee and making their own brand.

So Spruance turned to me and said, "Will you try some of my coffee, or will you drink the slop that my staff gets out of the pantry?"

I said, "I've heard about your coffee. I'd like to try a sample.

The guy on the other side of me said, "You won't like it. It's awful."

Well, it was the strongest stuff I ever got hold of. It really curled my hair.

Spruance had a different method for breaking the war tension than Fitch, but a very effective one. In the general conversation going around the mess table, somebody used a two dollar word, and Spruance said, "Exactly what does that mean?" While he was struggling for a definition, somebody jumped up and ran across to get the unabridged dictionary, and was thumbing through to check up on him.

The chap on my left got in a good one. He worked into the conversation a kind of a ten syllable word, and the Old Man challenged him. He had the definition down pat. He'd looked it up just before dinner and then figured a way to work it in.

This word game was just one of the ways of getting away from the war, arguing about the word meanings. It was a regular game in that mess.

Later when I was working for Oldendorf ...

Q: Then did you go that night?

van Deurs: I stayed aboard that night. Art Davis said, "you can have my brass bed. I'm going to sleep up in the sea cabin."

She was steaming that night over to Okinawa, and the next morning I got in some kind of a craft they called alongside and went down through the anchorage and found the TENNESSEE, and reported to Oldendorf aboard her.

I found him up in the sea cabin in the bunk. She'd been shooting all night, preventive fire support for the troops, and he was trying to catch a little shut eye, when I introduced myself. I told him I didn't know why I was there, I didn't know anything about battleships.

He said, "I know all about battleships. But maybe this'll make you feel better," and picked up a dispatch that was on the night table. It said when van Deurs reports to give him a physical exam then make him a Commodore. Well, that was a little bit better.

Then he went on to tell me that King had issued an order that any task force commander who didn't wear wings had to have a Chief of Staff that did. If a force commander wore wings, he had to have a Chief of Staff that did not.

After Surigao, Oldendorf, and his Chief of Staff, had gone to Washington for a conference. The Admiral went to King's office and asked Edwards, who was King's Chief of Staff, "I don't want to change Chief of Staff, I've got one I like very much right now. What will happen if I go in and ask Ernie to keep the man I've got?"

Edwards said, "It'll come right off at the neck."

"All right, I won't ask him. But I don't know any aviators ..."

He went down the corridor to Fitch who was then Chief of Bureau and asked Fitch. "The only aviator I know is Eddie Ewens, should I get him?"

Fitch said, "No. You get van Deurs."

This had happened while I was at Seattle, and somehow the orders didn't get out in time to stop me from taking the ship out again, so I had a little bit of extra fun.

Oldendorf had gone back to Ulithi to get on his flagship. Scrappy Kessing had talked to him, and Rafe Bates, his Chief of Staff into having dinner in his camp before they went out to the ship. They did.

Started to the ship in the dark in one of those little skimmer boats we had, little personnel boat that was very lightweight, would make about twenty-five or thirty knots if you opened it up. They told the coxswain to take it easy, they weren't in any hurry, take it slow going out there and not hit anything. The harbor was all dark. The damn fool opened this thing wide up and ran smack into a big steel navigation buoy, smashed the boat all to pieces. Threw Oley against the forward part of the cockpit, broke all his ribs on one side, and banged up Bates, the Chief of Staff, somewhat less.

So instead of getting aboard the TENNESSEE to make the assault he ended up in the hospital on Guam, and managed to talk Nimitz into not reporting it to Washington. He was afraid Ernie would relieve him. Managed to keep it quiet.

Nimitz sent Admiral Deyo to run the bombardment force for the beginning of the assault with Oldendorf's staff. And Oley had just gotten back a few days before I reported over there.

I liked him very much. He was a nice fellow to serve with. I began liking him about the first afternoon or evening.

A whole flock of ships lay anchored in Naguchi anchorage. When the Japanese came down to raid the place the ships orders were not to use any anti-aircraft guns in the anchorage. They had smoke boats stationed all around the perimeter. When the radar said planes were coming in, the boats began making artificial smoke that covered the whole place so you couldn't see anything at all.

Oldendorf, a great big tall chief quartermaster, and I were standing on the flag bridge, just staring out into the smoke.

We heard planes overhead; couldn't see 'em. The ship had been hit a few days before by a Kamikaze, that knocked one of her gun mounts off, so people were a little bit touchy. Standing there leaning on the splinter shield - the island or the mast structure was rectangular, but the splinter shield was round, so that at the corners there was just a narrow passageway wide enough for a thin man. We heard a plane go into a dive, couldn't see it at all in the smoke. But it sounded like it was coming right for us, and the same idea hit all three of us at the same time - that the other side of the bridge would be an awful good place to be. Nobody said anything but we all started at the same time. Oley and the big quartermaster hit the narrow corner at the same time and ended up on their hands and knees wedged in there with their fannies sticking up towards me. I went flat on the deck behind them. There was no place else to go.

The bomb or Kamikaze went boom in the water somewhere between us and the next ship. We got up and dusted ourselves off, looking kind of foolish, and laughed about it. Oley thought it was funnier'n the dickens, so I kind of liked him from there on. He didn't get fussed at all no matter what happened.

But a peculair experience - the man I was to relieve was at least six years senior to me. I mean he was class of '13. He was a very smart man, and he knew it, and he really considered himself the greatest strategist since Nelson or maybe before. He talked an awful lot, blowing his own horn. He was always kicking because he'd been passed over and all his classmates were admirals long before that, and he was still a captain, and a bachelor.

Q: You had trouble with a guy like that before - Pete Beck.

van Deurs: Oh no, Rafe Bates was not like Pete Beck.

He was a bachelor and a black shoe guy and he didn't particularly like aviators. I'd never seen him before and he had no reason to love me, and I was junior to him. I came aboard and was made a Commodore immediately and hence was senior to him. And I was taking a job that he liked.

He was ordered to command PT boats down in the Philippines or something, and I had the word that he'd be a commodore as soon as he got there, but he wouldn't believe it. Eventually it did happen.

For about a month we overlapped on the ship there. There was a working agreement between us. I took over the operations that were going on. Rafe still had a lot of reports to write from previous operations. He put up with me. He didn't have any reason to love me. I could understand the position very well.

But he did me a great favor. Under Oldendorf were half a dozen rear admirals and a whole flock of battleships captains and so on, none of whom I knew at all. Bates got me one afternoon and sat down and gave me a thumbnail sketch of each one of these people, and he was extremely accurate. "This man can do so and so, but he can't be trusted to do that, and this man has a certain peculiarity, another man has another one," and so on down the line. He was extremely accurate and completely honest in the opinions he gave me, and as time went on I found they were extremely valuable.

Then he gave me the dope on Oldendorf, which was worth more than all the rest of it. He said, "In the first place, Oley is not an idea man. You've got to generate all the ideas, and then you'll get surprised because you will propose something to the Admiral, on account of because thus and so, it seems like a good idea, and a couple of hours later he'll send for you and tell you to do this on account of thus and so, as if it was his idea and he'd just thought of it. The first time it happened to me I dropped my teeth. I couldn't understand. He quoted me right back to myself.

"It will happen to you. I don't think he realizes he does it, but it will happen every time, and you've just got to roll with it and pretend it never happened."

Q: That would be hard to do.

van Deurs: No, it was very easy.

A dispatch would come in from Spruance or Nimitz or somebody. I'd look at the thing and decide what seemed like a good idea to me, and I'd walk into the Admiral's cabin and say, "Admiral, I suggest that we do thus and so." We'd talk about it a few minutes; I'd give him my reasons and go on out. Send for whoever on the staff had to do the work and say, "Get going, we're going to do this and that, get it set up."

About an hour later the Admiral would send an orderly over, he wanted to see me. I'd go over. "I've got this thing from Nimitz, I think we ought to do this and that, so and so," and quote all my reasons back to me. And I'd say, "Yes, Admiral, I thought you'd want to do that. I've got that already started."

Q: He wanted the ideas, no question about that.

van Deurs: Oh, he wanted the ideas, no doubt about that.

Q: Didn't you ever say to him, "That's what I told you an hour ago?"

van Deurs: No, I never did. The temptation was there, but I never did.

He'd do it with a perfectly straight face. I don't believe he realized what he was doing. He'd be mulling the thing over and it would come out word for word.

Q: Being forewarned, of course ...

van Deurs: Yes. Rafe Bates tipped me off to that, or I would have said something like, "I told you an hour ago." But that went on month after month. It was just a regular act.

After one operation we came back to Buckner Bay and Spruance was in there. The Admiral took me over to call on the Old Man. I think he was in one of the fast battleships by that time. Went aboard, sat down, had a cup of coffee. Spruance told some funny stories.

Q: Did he really?

van Deurs: Yes, interesting chitchat.

Q: I never attributed a funny story to Admiral Spruance.

van Deurs: No, he told several very good stories. I got a chuckle out of them. I've forgotten what they were now.

After about twenty minutes Oley said, "Well, thanks for the coffee," and so on, time to go, got up and we walked out. As we started down the gangway Oley said, "Well, now we have our orders, we know what we've got to do."

I said, "Orders? I didn't hear any orders."

"Oh," he said, "you aren't wise. A lot of guys have gotten fired because they didn't understand Spruance's stories, but you think about it. Every one of those stories had a point. He was telling us what he wanted us to do. Now we're going to do it."

That was it. It was general instructions. They came out of these little stories, anecdotes.

Q: I'm glad he understood.

van Deurs: We went along that way for a month on the basis of that. That was one I would have completely missed, if I hadn't had Oldendorf's guidance on that one, because I thought - gee, the bird has got a little bit of small talk, very social meeting, and it wasn't at all. Those were the instructions.

Q: I wish you could remember his stories.

van Deurs: I can't remember a one of them. But a very pleasant way of doing business, but ...

Q: You'd have to be clever to figure that out.

What was the mission of the TENNESSEE while you were on her?

van Deurs: The fighting was still going on on Okinawa. Oldendorf's command was the bombardment force. It included all the old battleships and some other things. His administrative job was Commander Battleship Squadron One, which included all the old battleships, but as the task force commander he was boss of everything that was bombarding Okinawa. We had a whole flock of cruisers, rocket ships, gunboats....

Q: Oh, everything, all the bombardment.

van Deurs: Yes, all the bombardment from the sea.

The way it worked - by that time the troops were fighting pretty hard on the south end of Okinawa, and it was pretty rough terrain, sort of sawtooth. They'd take one ridge, go down and end up in a valley facing a cliff that was full of fortifications and artillery dug into caves and so on that had to be reduced. They used ship's guns and air, bombs, rockets, and everything else to try to blast the Japs out. It was one ridge after another. It was pretty tough going. Fortunately Okinawa wasn't very wide. The battleships's guns could shoot clear across the island. The sea was calm, so that you could stop a ship here and put the shells wherever you wanted. With each of the Army and Marine units fighting there were forward observers, Navy people with a radio set. They talked directly to the plotting room of the ship that was told to support their units. Each day the ships were assigned certain places and to support certain units ashore. They got in direct communication with this forward observer. Both had a grid map of the place. The observer would say they wanted so many shells planted at so and so, and the ship's plotting room crew would turn the guns around and deliver the shells as ordered. A lot of times there'd be a crossroads, say. They wanted to keep the Japs from moving through at night, so they asked for a shell every two minutes or every three minutes over a certain crossroads.

Q: They'd bombard day and night?

van Deurs: Day and night. Believe it or not, it got so I could sleep in a sea cabin with the ports open with a turret right outside and the turret going off every two minutes all night.

Q: Big guns?

van Deurs: Fourteen inch.

Q: Oh boy, I would think your hearing would have been absolutely ruined.

van Deurs: That's part of the reason I wear this thing.

Q: Oh, it started then?

van Deurs: Well that helped it. The airplanes for years, largely open face airplanes, started it, but I think the bombardment put the frosting on it.

Before I went over there I said to Art Davis, "What do you do if they're shooting all night and you don't get any sleep?"

Davis said, "Oh hell, you turn in. The first one goes off, you come right out of the bunk and land on the floor. The next one, you'll sit up in the bunk. The third one, you may open an eye. And after that you'll sleep right through it."

And he was quite correct. You got so as long as they were shooting regular, why you didn't notice it. You could sleep right through it.

Q: Kamikazes coming at you every day?

van Deurs: The picket ships caught most of the Kamikazes. They very seldom got through to the transport area or where the fighting was going on. They weren't well enough trained. They were sent down to get the big ships, but most of them dove at the first thing they saw. We lot a lot of destroyers and a lot of small craft that were on picket station out there to give warning of raids. They were the ones that caught hell from the Kamikazes, more than we did. Very few of them ever got through to the big ships. The TENNESSEE had taken one just before I got aboard, but that was more or less of a rare occasion.

Q: How long were you on the TENNESSEE?

4 van Deurs 537

van Deurs: Till after the end of the war.

Somewhere in there we took her back to Ulithi to get the gun mount replaced. That was maybe a month after I went aboard. Rafe Bates got off down there, went on to his next job. I guess Okinawa was secured very shortly after we got back and the fighting was over.

The Japanese had laid a whole flock of mines in the China Sea between Okinawa and China. One of the agreements Roosevelt had made with the Russians at Yalta was that we would supply Vladivostok.

While we were fighting at Okinawa they punched one convoy right through the Kurile Islands, with a lot of air support and gun ships. They ran it right through the Kurile Islands, and then to Vladivostok When the ice would close that route thay planned to go through Tsushi Straits. The idea was to clear out the mines from the China Sea so that the big carriers could go in there. Then they could take a convoy, run it through between Japan and Korea there, with all the air cover that was necessary to just smash down any opposition from either Korea or Japan.

There was a big force of minesweepers sent out to clear the China Sea, and Oldendorf with a lot of his ships and some of the small carriers were sent out there to keep the Japanese planes off the minesweepers. For a good part of the summer after Okinawa was secured, we were steaming around the China Sea, guarding the sweepers that were cleaning out the mines. We had I guess a division of the small carriers with us and several cruisers and battleships to do the anti-aircraft fire.

Q: What were the Japs able to do with planes at that time?

van Deurs: Oh, they still had a few planes coming down. Didn't bother us seriously, condition Red a few times there.

Q: Did you miss being on a carrier with the flying?

van Deurs: Yes, in a way, and still I enjoyed working for Oldendorf. It was very interesting, particularly with his personality. It was very pleasant. I had no problems. We got along very well.

Q: Where were you on V-J day?

van Deurs: When the first atom bomb let go, we were out in the China Sea. We got a message that on a certain date be sure that there were no planes or ships within fifty miles of two or three different locations - we didn't know what that meant. Next thing we heard that Hiroshima was flat.

Then Nimitz sent for Oldendorf to come down to Guam on a conference, on more or less what to do next. The planning had been going on; we'd been working on it; we had two or three plans for after Okinawa. One was to make a landing in China and lick the Japanese Army in China, and then go from China to Japan. Another called for, I think it was considered going into Korea, but that never got very serious. The other was for a direct landing in Kyushu, the southern Japanese island.

Apparently the high command couldn't make up its mind which to do. We'd get orders to go to work on the China deal and then we'd get orders to put that on ice and go to work on the Kyushu deal. They worked back and forth on those plans.

After Hiroshima Nimitz called a conference of his admirals down at Guam. By that time an old friend of mine, Admiral John Dale Price, was running our naval aviation on Okinawa. We had several fields over there. I got a plane from John, some kind of a fancy DC that was fixed up with bunks. We took off at night and Oley and I had a good nights sleep going to Guam in a very comfortable bunk in this plane that John gave us.

Q: Did you get in on the conference?

van Deurs: Yes. We were down there for a couple of days talking this thing over. Before any conclusions were reached Forrest Sherman came in one day - I guess he was Nimitz's operations officer - and said, "We ought to hear something in the next ten minutes, I guess." "What?" "Well, the boys are up there now to let another one go." That was the afternoon they knocked Nagasaki off the map.

Somebody said, "Hey Forrest, how many of those things have we got, anyway?" Sherman just held up two fingers. That was all the atom bombs we had actually.

Q: You think that was true?

van Deurs: Yes. We just had two of them. They'd made three up to that time. They let one go in the desert out here, and the two we dropped on Japan - those were the only ones that were built.

Q: I wonder if the Japanese knew this - of course not...

van Deurs: Nobody knew it.

Q: Except Forrest Sherman and you.

van Deurs: A few guys in Washington and Los Alamos and the Manhattan Project. They were working on others, but hadn't made enough plutomium to make any more yet.

Q: Can you describe the conference?

van Deurs: The conference broke up with thinking the war was about ended, that they would cave in in the next few days. If not, we'd go ahead with the landing plan at Kyushu.

We flew back to Okinawa. Soon things quieted down and we got orders to send all the old battleships that had been doing the bombardment there for months to send them down to the Philippines for leave, let them have a little blow, for the staff to move into the PENNSYLVANIA which was on her way out from the States after battle repairs. She was due in a couple of days. She came into Okinawa about the time there was a false rumor that there was peace, and the Army went wild on the beach shooting off everything they had.

The PENNSYLVANIA came alongside the TENNESSEE. We loaded the staff into it, then told her to anchor out on the edge of the flock of ships that were anchored in Buckner Bay. We didn't think it worth making other people move. The TENNESSEE and the other ships were going out next morning, and after they left we planned to move in closer to the beach in a good anchorage.

Some of the staff, enlisted men, were arguing about the move before the PENNSYLVANIA arrived - she will be the next ship hit, it always happens, ship gets hit once, she goes back to the States, she comes back, she's just monkey meat, she'll get hit again right away.

That night I walked up on deck. There were lights showing all over the ship. There were cracks and clinks and so on, a lot of lights over on the beach, but all the ships were blacked out. I sent for the exec and told him that the God damn war was still on, to get his ship blacked out and be quick about it. And he did; got the lights out. I went back down below.

She'd been fitted as a flagship originally. The Admiral's cabin was a great big place that once had a lot of nice ports in it, with a five inch gun mounted there. Now the gun casement and ports were all welded shut. It was just a tin box. Somebody had fitted it with a lot of iron garden furniture, little tables and chairs like that, all over. He looked at those things and made some sarcastic remarks about the decorations. The ships were depressing to live in. There was no paint on the bulkheads, fire you know, and it was just like being inside of a sardine can, and this garden furniture looked pretty ridiculous in such a cabin. It wouldn't burn, that was the only thing you could say about it. There was a big desk against the after bulkhead.

The captain's cabin was across the aisle from the Old Man's in the stern and just forward of that was a big cabin for the CHief of Staff, a desk against the after bulkhead and a big round table, a dining room table, anchored in the middle of it.

About eight o'clock I was sitting at the desk trying to plow through the stack of mail she had brought, and a torpedo got us. I didn't know what it was at first, but the whole place was full of smoke and the deck jumping up and down like a springboard. The shock of the thing, I never figured out how I landed on my feet on the other side of this round table that had been behind me. The overhead wasn't very high. I didn't touch anything, twisted my back in doing it, sprained it very badly - it still gives me trouble occasionally.

Q: The shock threw you.

van Deurs: Yes, this thing threw me right out of the desk chair, somersault, backwards, and landed on my feet. I stuck my head out the door and asked the orderly, "What the hell was that?" and he said, "I didn't do it, sir! It wasn't here."

It was funny - the ship was full of grey smoke. You could smell the explosive, and yet it had hit on the flat of the bottom several decks down. She was buttoned up, all the armor closed, and everything, but it permeated the whole darned thing.

Q: Did it explode?

van Deurs: Oh yes, it exploded. It blew the bottom out of the steering engine room, killed all the quartermasters who lived down there, knocked two of the propeller shafts off. I think it hit one of the propeller shafts; flooded one engine.

I bounced up on a ladder onto the quarterdeck, and the water was standing on the quarterdeck right up to the hatch combing, over my shoes.

There was no general alarm, no nothing. I went up over the upper decks to the forward island structure and climbed up to where the radio was and the flag plot. Some of the other staff did the same thing. I looked around, and the ship's people weren't doing anything. So we told them -- as I went through the upper deck in the dark various sailors recognized an officer and said, "What shall we do sir? Shall we go to battle stations?" I said, yes, go to the stations. When I got up on the bridge I sounded the alarm, and began to ask what damage reports the officer of the deck was getting. Well, first it didn't look too bad.

Q: Who was the skipper of the ship?

van Deurs: The skipper of the ship was a man named Moses.

Q: Hadn't he done anything?

van Deurs: He hadn't done anything. He was back in his cabin, and he hadn't done anything.

Q: How could that be?

van Deurs: Of course on a flagship the radio belongs to the flag. They take over the ship's radio as soon as they go aboard.

Q: Yes, but battle stations and damage to the ship ...

van Deurs: That was the skipper's business.

I told the officer of the deck or somebody to sound the general alarm and get people to stations that way, and got the damage reports.

She was an old ship, riveted construction, and this thing had gone off under the flat of the stern and the whole ship had gone like a springboard. She whipped and pulled rivets loose all through the ship, so that none of the watertight bulkheads held, and the first reports that came up there - we only had a couple of flooded compartments, didn't sound serious.

But as time went on, why, it leaked through. Compartments that had been reported dry an hour before were flooded. Before it got very far I got on the radio, called the service force flagship up at the other end of the Bay, told them to send a lot of salvage tugs down, that we'd been hit. Then I started looking around a little.

The Admiral hadn't showed up so I sent one of his staff down to see if he was all right. What had happened to Oley - he'd been sitting at the desk writing a letter to his wife, pulled open the drawer and leaned back in his chair to get another sheet of paper - this thing blew him out of the chair. It was right under both of the cabins, really. He landed spreadeagled on the deck, and all this garden furniture came down on top of him. He was just barely getting over his broken ribs and so on. It didn't do him a bit of good. It didn't put him out of action, but it didn't do him any good. We got him out of there.

Q: Was he able to navigate?

4 van Deurs - 545

van Deurs: Oh, yes. He was up on the bridge inside of a few minutes. The ship's skipper across the aisle also got bounced out of his cabin, but he put himself on the list for a Purple Heart for it!

Q: He must have been some kind of a nut.

van Deurs: I didn't know. He was the class ahead of me at the Naval Academy, but I never had known him there. I think he'd just taken the ship before she started out there. I don't know whether he'd had any combat experience before or not.

Q: Even I would know you order people to general quarters and find out what's going on!

van Deurs: There were some funny angles to the thing.

The reports kept getting worse. The salvage tugs got down and began helping to pump things out. One after another the reports were coming in of compartments flooded. A Marine orderly came in and said, "We just moved all your stuff up in the sea cabin, sir, yours and the Admiral's." "Why?" "Well, it's getting pretty wet back there where you live." "How about the rest of the staff?" They didn't know, so I sent them back to help move the other staff members' clothes and stuff up out of it.

One of these Marines just stood watch as my orderly. He was one of these wise guy operators. He was the kind of a guy that when he saw something new in the canteen he'd say, "The Commodore wants two of those," and then come tell me I ought to have one, they only cost fifty cents or a dollar or something, but he'd gotten his too! He was just the big operator type and kind of a loud-mouthed kid who amused me.

I said, "Where were you when this thing hit?"

"Oh," he said, "I was sitting on the bits back on the quarterdeck telling these boots about the war. They all just came out from the States. They didn't know anything about the war. I was telling them what it was like.

"I saw that plane coming. I was telling them, 'Now listen to that, that's one of our TBDs. They all sound like that. One of our torpedo planes – they always sound like that, see.'

"And then when I picked myself up out of the waterways ..."

It must have been one of the Japs' last good pilots, because it came from the direction of Formosa. The Air Force had a radar to go on the south end of Okinawa, but they'd never gotten around to putting it up. We'd had so many destroyers hit that we'd taken them off the picket station on the south end. This bird apparently flew up from the south, close to the water. Buckner Bay was bounded by a big coral reef, semicircular thing, always had surf on it, and he apparently flew along this line of surf until he saw the first big ship silhouetted against the Army lights on the beach. Then he turned in for the ship, turned on his running lights, – the air was full of American planes going in and out of the field – flew over a couple of destroyers at about a hundred feet with his running lights on, dropped the torpedo, turned around, flew out of the place, and when he got to the reef he turned off his running lights and went back to Fromosa or wherever he came from -- without anybody laying a gun on him or sounding an alarm or anything else. A perfect job - I don't know who he was but he knew his stuff, and he made a beautiful hit on the PENNSYLVANIA that put her out of commission.

The next morning we called a boat alongside and moved the staff back into the TENNESSEE and sent the other ships on their way. When you left you stepped up from the quarterdeck to get into the boat. The quarterdeck was just awash.

Q: Was she salvaged? She didn't go down, did she?

van Deurs: No, they managed to keep her afloat. We moved her in close to the beach in shallow water where she couldn't sink all the way, and they put some coffer dams in her and pumped her out, towed her back to the States. They had an awful job doing it because her rudder was jammed. Her steering gear was all wrecked in the explosion. But they managed to tow her back to Bremerton, then towed her to Bikini for a target.

There were a lot of suggestions. One suggestion right after she was hit was that we fill her full of concrete and use her as a defense battery at Okinawa. We'd been walking around fortifications for four or five years by that time. You went where the guns weren't. You did not have to walk into the guns put up for harbor defense. Everybody out there knew that harbor forts were finished. But somebody in Washington sent that dispatch out.

Q: Oh, really, seriously?

van Deurs: Yes, somebody sent that out. I don't know who it was. Naturally it didn't happen; nobody out there would agree.

My cruise on the PENNSYLVANIA was very short!

Q: But active.

van Deurs: Yes, active.

Our operations officer, a submariner, had done a remarkable job in the early part of the war as a submarine skipper, gotten all the medals. As a submariner on war patrol he'd gotten the practice of taking spares on each cruise.

For instance – on one cruise his watch went bad and he had a hell of a time, so when he got back to Pearl he bought three watches – wore one, and carried spares. His feet hurt, so there was only one kind of rather expensive shoes that would fit, so he'd have about three or four pairs of those that he'd never had on, they were spares –– everything accordingly.

He said he always took these spares with him after that on a submarine patrol. He said if the submarine got sunk it didn't make any difference. If they got back from the patrol and he hadn't used all the spares, they were good for the next trip. There wasn't much chance on a submarine of anybody surviving if the boat was lost, but he hadn't thought of that. When he came to Oldendorf's staff he brought along all his spares.

So we got off the PENNSYLVANIA without losing anything, except that getting off that morning we had to climb over a couple of salvage tugs to get to the boat. Men were passing the baggage and the files across. Everything got across except one bag got dropped, went down between two ships that came together and scrunched it and it was gone - that included all the operations officer's spare shoes and spare watches. It was the only thing that was lost.

After the Japanese promised to surrender, not too long after we went back to the TENNESSEE, we sent cruisers and hospital ships to various Japanese ports to bring out prisoners of war. Oldendorf was anxious to see how they were making out. As soon as the cease fire came, the ships began flying admirals' personal flags again, which had not been done during the war. Oldendorf as a vice admiral was the senior officer present in Buckner Bay, but task groups were coming in and out all the time. We were getting ready to dash into Korea to try to stop the Russians from taking all of the place, and there were various other groups moving in and out. Nobody knew quite what was there, but there were probably a thousand or two thousand ships of various types around Okinawa.

Q: How many?

van Deurs: A thousand, maybe more.

Oldendorf and my old friend, John Dale Price, who was running the naval air over on the island, took a seaplane and flew up to Wakiyama to see how this prisoner of war business was going on. Then they flew on over to Nagasaki, I believe, which was another port where we had rescue ships. Then, Navy regulations said, when an admiral left a ship if he was going to be gone less than seventy-two hours he had an option. He could either turn over the command to the next senior officer, which in this case would have been one of the rear admirals working for him, or he could keep his flag flying and let the Chief of Staff run the operation till he got back. If he was going to be gone more than seventy-two hours he was supposed to turn over to the next senior. Oldendorf said they'd get back in less than seventy-two, to keep the three stars flying, and for me to do it. It looked like a perfectly routine operation.

Q: Where were you geographically?

van Deurs: In Buckner Bay, Okinawa, Nagugasaki Wan, until General Buckner got shot and then they changed the name.

But while Oley was up in Japan a typhoon headed for Okinawa, and the typhoon warnings grounded him at Nagasaki. They couldn't get back.

Some time before I'd talked the Admiral into getting an aerologist on the staff. The one they sent had been a civil engineer down in Texas before the war and was a pretty serious minded youngster who had learned his aerology pretty well. He worked the weather map. The typhoon plotted as coming north and heading right for Okinawa. But the question was - would it curve before or after it hit?

There were two evacuation plans for typhoons. One said all the ships in the area headed east in parallel courses. The other one called for them to go through the passes between the islands and head west out into the China Sea on parallel courses. There was no way to change from one to the other. If you once started all these ships — as I say, there were between one and two thousand ships of various sizes and kinds — there was no possible way to reverse it without having a flock of collisions, or worse.

So I sent out the signal that got everybody ready to leave on short notice. Everybody had steam at the throttel, but I didn't know whether to go east or west. It was shortly after Halsey had lost a couple of destroyers by being caught on the wrong side of a typhoon in the dangerous semicircle.

As the aerologist and I watched this thing, I thought it was kind of funny — there were rear admiral flags flying all around the Bay, but not a darned one of them came over to confer with Oldendorf or offer any suggestions or any help. Finally, a flock of carriers came in flying a rear admiral's flag; that rear admiral came over. It was Art Davis, my old friend. He hit the quarterdeck, wanted to know where the Admiral was, and I told him he was up in Japan and I wished he was here. I told him about our dope on the typhoon. I took him down and showed him the maps we had and told him what I was waiting for.

He looked it over and said, "Well, you've got more dope and better dope than I have. Anything you do, I'll back you up." But he was the only one of a dozen admirals that were around there that came over to offer the Old Man any help. None of the others did.

Q: It's kind of sad, isn't it.

van Deurs: I thought it was rather low at the time. They didn't want any responsibility. Of course they did not know Oley was away.

Q: They didn't want to get in on any joint responsibility.

van Deurs: That was it. It was dodging responsibility.

The nets were still across Buckner Bay. There was just a narrow entrance for one ship to go through and no lights on it, so that you couldn't empty the place at night.

Q: What time of day was this?

van Deurs: It was in the afternoon, and you couldn't go out of the place at night. By the time it was getting dark we still didn't know which way this thing was going, but it looked like it couldn't possibly get there till the next afternoon. It was moving fairly slowly.

Q: How did you get these reports?

van Deurs: They'd started the typhoon tracking system, more or less. We were getting reports from Guam and the Philippines, various other places.

Q: Ships in the area too?

van Deurs: By radio.

I turned in but was up at daylight - I guess about five in the morning. The typhoon had speeded up during the night. When I popped up on deck on the TENNESSEE, anchored in Buckner Bay, the seas in the Bay were running right level with the quarterdeck, and the wind was really howling. I took one last look at the chart and sent the signal to go west. As I say, everybody was awful anxious to get out of there, but nobody was offering any suggestions or anything, and the minute we sent out the signal everybody started.

The opening in the nets was supposed to take one ship. When the TENNESSEE went through there were three battleships abreast going through that hole! People were that anxious to get out of there

Of course there were a certain number of ships that had their engines disabled one way or another. They couldn't move. They were alongside of repair ships. Most of them were wrecked in Buckner Bay

As we went out through the nets we met a whole flock of little minesweepers that were trying to get in. Somebody had let them start from Saipan without telling them there was a typhoon, and we didn't know they were coming. Around on the other side of Okinawa were a couple of coves that the small craft were supposed to take refuge in. They were pretty secure anchorages for very small ships. So as I went out through the nets I signalled these people to go around the island to the small craft anchorage. Some of them made it and some of them didn't. A couple of them capsized trying to turn around the north end of the island and were lost - I don't know how many.

Most people got in the open, got around through the islands, went in to the China Sea and rode the thing out. A couple of days later we turned around and came back in.

Q: So you had evaluated, thank God, the way the typhoon was going.

van Deurs: With the help of this kid aerologist, who guessed right on the thing.

Q: You weren't really guessing; you were really taking an evaluated judgment.

Van Deurs: The best information we had, put it that way.

Q: How high did the seas run where you were?

van Deurs: Oh, I don't know. I never did know how to judge the height of a sea. It was breaking over a battleship's bow and so on.

Q: All the ships rode it out?

van Deurs: Oh, yes. Almost any ship can ride out a typhoon if they've got sea room. We weren't going fast. We weren't pounding into it.

When we turned around and went back, Okinawa was knocked completely flat. The Army had dumped tons of lumber and stuff ashore there and set up a lot of quonset huts and so on, but nobody had anchored anything for a typhoon, and of course that all took off, and what didn't fly through the air got wrecked by things that did. I don't think there was a building standing, or any material left. It was a pretty sad sight.

Q: There wouldn't have been a ship left if you hadn't made the proper decision.

van Deurs: Some of the ships that were left at Buckner Bay, because they were disabled, were up on the beach.

When Oley and John Dale got back, John Dale was pretty disturbed when he saw his air stations and so on completely flat. He was all for abandoning it.

Since then they've made a permanent base there. They've made typhoon-proof buildings.

Q: What did Admiral Oldendorf say to you?

van Deurs: Oh, he approved of what we'd done; it suited him fine.

Q: I'm sure it did.

van Deurs: He had no kick.

Q: Maybe that together with the other operations that you had is responsible for your receiving a Letter of Commendation from the Commander of the Fifth Fleet. It was Fifth Fleet then?

van Deurs: Yes, that was Fifth Fleet.

Q: Bronze Star Commendation ribbon awarded the TENNESSEE for her splendid record.

van Deurs: That was the TENNESSEE.

They had a system that if you were in a ship that got a Unit Citation, either Presidential or Navy, you were wearing a ribbon for that citation from then on.

The CHENANGO had the Navy citation.

Q: Navy Unit Citation.

van Deurs: And the TENNESSEE did too, I think.

If you were in the ship when she won it you wore the ribbon permanently. If it got aboard after that, you wore it as long as you were attached to it - I think that was the rule. In other words her crew wore it.

The CHANANGO had two citations and the TENNESSEE had one. No, I thought it was the commendation ribbon that Spruance gave me for that Chief of Staff job I did.

Q: I don't have that actual reference. What did Spruance give you?

van Deurs: Commendation ribbon.

4 van Deurs - 557

Q: For you personally?

van Deurs: Yes.

Q: For you duty on the TENNESSEE?

van Deurs: For my work with Oldendorf; I think I've got it down below some place.

Q: I did want to comment that your house on this level doesn't show the Legion of Merit or any of your citations or awards.

van Deurs: They're in a drawer down in the lower room, also with some pieces of old uniform. I've never had much sympathy for those people that make out a showcase and put their medals in it, because most of the medals I got were earned by other people. I just happened to be the boss man or happened to be around.

Q: But you know that the only good thing any outfit does, civilian, Navy, or whatever, is because the boss is good.

van Deurs: I always felt that they were more decorations for my team than they were for me, so there's no reason for me to put them on display and boast about them.

Q: Just the same, you know basically the team is only as good as the boss.

van Deurs: Somewhere they made a mistake. I think the record shows that I rate a star, a second Legion of Merit.

Q: Right, second and third.

van Deurs: When they sent the second one they sent a medal by mistake. Tommy Sprague pinned it on me at Seattle, and I said, "I only rate a star, I don't rate one of these things." Tommy said, "The hell with that, they sent a medal and that's what you get."

So I think my daughter Sally pinched that one. She carried it around and had it on display in various places, for a long time, and that was the only one that ever was displayed.

Q: Tell me then about the evacuation of the prisoners. You participated in that ...

van Deurs: I didn't have anything directly to do with that, except that some of the ships that were sent up there were part of Oldendorf's command.

Q: Were you on any of the ships?

van Deurs: No, I never got in on that at all.

But they sent them into Tokyo and they sent them into the inland sea, to Wakiyama, and to Nagasaki, and maybe some places that I've forgotten. I know those three, and then they sent parties inland to wherever the camps were, to bring these people out. I didn't have anything to do with it. A lot of prisoners were in pretty bad shape. That's why they sent hospital ships in.

And there was one funny thing happened - after that typhoon, a destroyer coming back from Japan, had been up there on the evacuation, sighted a small Coast Guard patrol boat, one hundred ten footer, and flashed a signal at it, couldn't get any answer. They stopped and looked at it. It was dead in the water, wasn't going anywhere - in broad daylight, but the running lights were on. They didn't see anybody on deck, so the skipper lowered a boat and sent somebody to board the thing. There was nobody on board it. All the hatches were open. She was perfectly dry inside. She was a diesel ship and her diesel generator was still running and all the lights were on all over the ship. So they took it on in to Okinawa.

The Coast Guard first said they didn't know what it was. It was marked Coast Guard with a Coast Guard number on it, but the Coast Guard claimed it wasn't their ship, they didn't know anything about it at all.

Finally the story came out -- The night before we evacuated Buckner Bay for the typhoon, this thing was trying to go alongside a tender, with I think a chief petty officer in command. He made a pass at the tender, and one man jumped over with a line. The line slipped through his hand and she drifted out - the wind was pretty strong. Came around, made another pass, and another man jumped over with a line, and the line slipped out of his hand. I think the last time they went around the chief jumped over, and the boat went adrif

During the night it had drifted out of Buckner Bay and rode out the typhoon without anybody on board it, floated like a cork and didn't ship any water. She was dry and in perfectly good shape.

But the Coast Guard was too embarrassed to claim her for about a week.

We left Okinawa a week or so after that; left for the surrender. None of us could quite believe the Japs would actually quit like that, absolutely carry out the terms of the surrender. They'd just been fighting too hard for too long. We just couldn't believe that they could suddenly turn off the faucet.

So when the MISSOURI and the fast carriers and so on went into Tokyo Bay for surrender, there was another task force under Oldendorf just out of sight over the horizon which consisted of all the old battleships and a lot of the jeep carriers. We were loaded for bear just in case anybody pulled any kind of a doublecross.

Q: I never heard that before.

van Deurs: Well, we were there. That's why I didn't see the surrender on the MISSOURI because we were just out of sight waiting for some word that somebody had pulled a doublecross, and we were loaded to let them have everything there was if they did.

After that, we went in and covered the troop landings at all the different ports west of Tokyo. The first was Wakiyama, which is right at the eastern entrance to the Inland Sea. It was a funny show because the amphibious people had these ships all loaded for the assault on

Japan, and they insisted on making a combat landing just for practice, ran through the surf and so on. So Oldendorf and I and a couple of other people went ashore early to a boat landing in the town. Took a jeep and went around and got on some sand dunes out at the edge of the city where this landing was to take place and watched the amphibious landing from the enemy's side, as it were.

Q: That was really an experience, wasn't it?

van Deurs: When we went through the town everything was shuttered. There wasn't a Jap in sight. They were scared to death; thought they'd all be murdered right out. I think we landed a liberty party before the landing force took over, from the battleships and so on.

It went on for two or three days, then the shutters began to come down. People that were getting kind of hungry began coming out and began to barter and swap with the sailors when they saw that they weren't going to be assaulted or anything. Of course we had MPs and SPs and it was all perfectly orderly. The town gradually went back to normal.

We went on and put troops ashore at Kure, and the southern island, Shikoku, and then over at Nagasaki and Sasebo. Nagasaki was rather funny. The Second Marines were in there. A lot of the docks were not damaged. You could put a ship right alongside the dock. But the streets back of the docks were full of debris, and the Japanese were sitting on their ditty boxes starving to death, yet there were warehouses full of rice. They never looted the things. The town administration had completely gone to hell. The Marines could not get their equipment ashore through the blocked streets.

Q: It wasn't dangerous to go into Nagasaki?

van Deurs: What do you mean – from the bomb? No.

Q: No radiation?

van Deurs: Not enough to bother anybody.

The Marines took over the warehouse of rice and offered food to the people that would work; put them to work cleaning up the streets. They were perfectly willing to go to work and glad to be fed. They'd just been sort of dazed, doing nothing. The town administration had fallen apart and nobody was giving any orders, so they did nothing. The Marines had no trouble at all.

Nagasaki was built in a number of valleys. The harbor is sort of a short stemmed T, a beautiful thing, the entrance on the stem of the T. At the north end of it a valley went all up into the hills; the bomb went off over that valley, and that was completely cleaned out. There had been a big Mitsibishi plant in there making torepdoes, and I think steel. THat was knocked flat.

Q: Did you go into any of these places?

van Deurs: I went into all of them. Oh, the next ridge there were a few houses knocked off the ridge, but the next valley was practically undamaged. The part near the harbor, where this blast had come down the valley, had wrecked things near the waterfront. In back of that the town wasn't badly hurt.

The Marines eventually bulldozed a little landing strip at about ground zero that was big enough to take these little monoplane observation planes that the Army used for artillery control and so on.

Later when I was the SOP in Western Japan, people that wanted to see Nagasaki usually went to Sasebo. The Marines had a lot of these little planes and we would line up a flock of them. Each one would carry one passenger. It would take several hours to run from Sasebo to Nagasaki in a destroyer, but in about ten minutes you could get there in a plane and land on this atomic field. We used to fly all sightseeing expeditions for the visiting firemen.

Q: Now, at this time what was your status?

van Deurs: I was on the TENNESSEE as Chief of Staff.

After that, after we'd gotten all the troops ashore, we had an order from Washington, "When released send the TENNESSEE and CALIFORNIA to Philadelphia," by either Cape Horn or Good Hope, whichever was shortest. They had blisters built on them, they couldn't go through Panama, and King wouldn't pay the tolls to go through Suez because the British would not count them on return lend-lease, so he was stubborn, he wouldn't send anything through Suez.

I sat down with the chart and figured it out, where we were — the Inland Sea, I think, at that time. It was a few miles shorter by Good Hope. So I wrote out a long dispatch to the Navy Department recommending that we go via these ports, and I named every place in India and Africa that I ever wanted to see and never had seen, and Bahia, Brazil — thought it was worth a chance.

To my surprise they came back and said, "Approved, except substitute Rio for Bahia," which was a bit further west, and I hadn't had quite the crust to put it on. Gee, that was fine.

The Admiral said, "Turn the ships over to the senior commanding officer to run the show, and you can do your sunbathing over there, and I'll take this side to do my sunbathing, and we'll look forward to a gentlemen's cruise home."

Then another typhoon hit. We rode that one out in the Inland Sea at anchor. It wasn't too bad, except somewhere in the middle of it - it came along just in time to stop us in sailing - came along another radio saying, "Sail the TENNESSEE and CALIFORNIA under the senior commanding officer; Oldendorf and his staff move into some other ship and remain in Japan."

And the skipper of the TENNESSEE never even said, "Thank you," for the nice cruise I'd fixed him up with!

We moved into what had been one of the amphibious flagships, I think the APPLACHIAN, with a wonderful communications setup that we didn't need and so on, but it was available.

I guess before the typhoon, Spruance sent a message for Oldendorf to come over to Yokuska for a conference. I wrote out an answer saying, "Unless directed otherwise, I am proceeding with the TENNESSEE, CALIFORNIA, and all the battleships and cruisers and carriers that are working for us."

The Old Man said, "Why? We can get in an airplane and get over there very quickly."

I said, "Yes, but these kids have been fighting a war. They rate a look at Tokyo before they go home. Let's take them all along."

So he sent it. Spruance never said boo. We took the whole task force and went up Tokyo Bay and turned the kids loose.

Q: They sure did deserve a look. That was extremely thoughtful of you.

van Deurs: Spruance was very gracious and very nice, and turned over his car and chauffeur to show us the ruins of Tokyo and Yokohama. We had a very enjoyable day doing that.

Also, before or after that, he invited us to go for a walk with him in the afternoon. You may have heard of Spruance's walks. He did a heel and toe business that carried him along at about five miles an hour and he could keep it up all afternoon. He loved to just go straight across everything. Some of his staff could stay with him, but most of them couldn't. He'd walk the legs off any of them.

I made some kind of an excuse. I ended up in the Yokuska Club drinking beer. Oley started out, but he was one of a whole flock of them that dropped by the wayside long before Spruance was ready to turn around and head back. Oley came into the Club late in the afternoon looking like he'd been through a wringer. Spruance was still stepping out, having himself a swell time.

Q: How did you feel when you saw Tokyo, the city that had been the enemy for all these years?

van Deurs: It was a marvelous wreck. What most people didn't realize is, a lot more people died one night in Tokyo then ever died in Hiroshima. There was a fire raid put on by several hundred B-24s, and it happened to be a windy night. The fires started just behind the waterfront of Yokohama, back of the docks. The docks were not harmed, but in back of the docks, from there to the Imperial Palace in Toyko, there was nothing left standing, just completely burned out. Nobody ever knew exactly how many people died because people trying to run ahead of the fire got caught in dead end streets, things like that, and the bodies were piled up twenty feet deep.

Q: Any evidences of that when you saw it?

van Deurs: Oh, the place hadn't been fixed up at all. The bodies were gone, but there was nothing. There were only two things between the waterfront at Yokohama and the moat at the Imperial Palace that were higher than my knee, and those were the concrete chimneys that had been on the bath houses, and the iron safes.

The iron safes were quite a joke, because Japan towards the tail end of the war had collected all the scrap iron and scrap steel they could to make munitions, and all the Japanese merchants swore they'd turned in their safes for scrap metal, because Japan was honest and they didn't really need a safe, but when this fire cleaned out the place, these safes were standing up like monuments all over the place. Most hadn't turned them in, and most of them were perfectly good safes except they had tin backs, and somebody had looted the things by opening the back with a can opener after the fire.

Q: I never knew that.

van Deurs: It was the darnedest wreckage you ever saw. I was in Hiroshima and Nagasaki both, but this thing was just as flat, and a hell of a lot more people died in Yokohama and Tokyo than died in either of the other two places. The only difference was, it took one plane to do the damage at Hiroshima and it took a flock of planes to do it at Yokohama and Tokyo, but it was just as complete. It was one of the biggest slum clearance jobs that was ever done.

Q: So we could have done over Japan probably without the atomic bomb anyway.

van Deurs: We probably could have.

Actually I believe it's on the record that the Japanese asked the Russians to get a peace offer from us in May. The Russians sat on it, never passed it along, so that we didn't know it.

The Navy pretty well felt that Japan would either surrender without being invaded, because we were starving them out, or that we could land on Kyushu without too many losses. The Army thought it was going to be awfully tough. They estimated the losses in millions and wanted all the help they could get. They may have been wrong, I don't know. The Army certainly was over-estimating the casualties, because the aerial photographs they had of Kyushu looked like they were putting beach defenses all over the place.

After we got in there I flew all over the place looking over the thing, and most of these things that looked like serious trenchworks and beach defenses were dummies - just sand dunes, dummy airplanes and dummy artillery pieces made out of straw, and things like that. But they photographed and looked tough. By the time we got there they didn't have anything to defend with - completely out of gasoline, oil, metals, everything that was necessary to keep going. But that of course is hindsight. At the time none of us knew it.

Finally - I don't know - we cruised back and forth visiting various western Japan ports. At Kure, the Army 41st Division staff took over a compound of little bungalows that had belonged to the Japanese army or air force. They set one cottage aside for the senior officer afloat, to come ashore and use for a drinking place if they wanted to. We were there two or three times.

Oldendorf and Admiral Riggs and I used to go ashore, take a walk, but send a boy over to the house with some whiskey and ice. We would hike through the hills, come back to this place and have a drink. We would usually send an invitation over to the General and some of his staff to come over and join us.

The first time the General said, "Come over and have a drink with us." They only had this Suntori whiskey. The Army had confiscated all there was. I don't know what it's like now, but it was awfully raw stuff then. It was horrible. We accepted their invitation just once. We managed to have some good American whiskey stowed away, so the arrangement suited them fine. They were delighted to come over and join us.

The wings I was wearing created a bit of conversation there because that division had been on the beach at Leyte, and the Air Force had flung a field down there, about a week or so after the landing. Shortly after the Battle of Leyte Gulf, they said they were ready to take over the troop support. The carriers could go home. Up to that time we had been doing it, and it had gotten to be quite a tough fight. There'd been an awful lot of air support missions flown from the little carrier. After the Air Force took over, we went home, and the Jap Air came back. They began giving our troops the devil, and the Air Force didn't have time for support missions. They were too busy defending their own airfield, so that it looked kind of bad. The only thing that saved the situation – when Halsey left the South Pacific, they left a Marine Air Wing on Bougainville, and somebody got the idea of yelling for them. They flew up to the Philippines, and they took over the troop support, for which they were well trained and had been practicing while the Air Force had never been trained for troops support. The Marine fliers got the Japanese off the soldiers' backs.

At Kure anybody who was wearing Navy wings could have anything those boys had. If an Air Force bird showed up, they wouldn't let him in the camp. They were the most pro-Navy-air people I ever met, and due largely to the fact that the carriers had taken care of them for the first couple of weeks and then the Marines had come in and saved their necks. They were very thankful for it.

The day came when we got a dispatch to dissolve the command and send the staff home. By that time Towers was commanding the Fifth Fleet; he'd taken Spruance's place.

A rear admiral who had been over in Sasebo, taking care of western Japan, was next senior to Oldendorf. He was going to take over for the whole area from Tokyo west. Little John Tom Bottom, who'd been the destroyer commodore for Oldendorf's task force during the war, was the Navy man at Nagoya. As soon as that order came out John Tom sent me a message, "Don't forget me, I want to go home too."

So I wrote out orders for Oldendorf, me, John Tom, and the rest of the staff, priority I Air to San Francisco and so on, and they looked very pretty, got them all signed. We went around to Tokyo to see Towers before we turned over.

Far Fahrion, the man that was to relieve Oldendorf, and I and Oley went over to see Towers. Oldendorf explained how we were making the turnover and all the details, going home and so on, and Towers turned around to the other man, "Does that suit you?"

"Yes, that's fine — except that I want van Deurs and Bottom. I want van Deurs to go over and take my place at Sasebo. I want Bottom to stay where he is."

I started to protest, "You can't do that to me," and said, "Well, you want a flag officer over there. The minute this staff dissolves I'm a captain again. I'm commissioned as a commodore just as long as I'm Oldendorf's Chief of Staff."

Towers, Oldendorf, and Fahrion all laughed like the dickens at me, at my protest, and Towers said, "Yeah, that's true. Well, we'll get you a new commission."

I said, "The war's over, they won't put out any more commodore commissions."

"Well, we'll try it."

I had a few more excuses. Every time I opened my mouth all three of them laughed at me. Towers sat down and wrote a dispatch and that evening I had a new commodore's commission for as long as I was in the Fifth Fleet.

So I kissed the rest of them good bye and they went home Priority One, and I got in a cruiser and went back to Sasebo to take over that part of the area.

Q: Was it fun being a commodore?

van Deurs: Not as much fun as being skipper of a carrier, but it was perfectly all right, being the head man around there. There wasn't much to do. Probably about six hundred ships that were there when I took over, a lot of them merchant ships that we were trying to get unloaded, send back home, and get them off the Navy's charter. I had a couple of cruisers I think and a squadron of destroyers.

Q: Was this when you became Commander Task Group 55.2 - Commander Naval Froces Kyushu?

van Deurs: Yes, that was it.

Q: In the cruiser OKLAHOMA CITY and later on the ATLANTA?

van Deurs: Yes.

Q: Only you were at Sasebo?

van Deurs: Yes, Sasebo was where I was most of the time, although I'd get tired of looking at Sasebo and go down to Kagashima or somewhere else.

Q: But you were aboard ship, first in the OKLAHOMA CITY and then the ATLANTA?

van Deurs: Yes, flying a flag in the cruiser. Both of them were commanded by classmates of mine. We were friends and it was a perfectly pleasant arrangement that way.

Q: Which ever ship you were on was the flagship at the time. What did you say — you went down to where, Kagasaki?

van Deurs: Kagashima; in some ways it was a very interesting city. It was the only stone city I ever saw in Japan. The buildings had all been built of masonry. It was down at the south end of Kyushu, near the north end of a long V-shaped bay, maybe twenty or thirty miles long, and right in front of this city was an island that was a volcano.

The first time I went in there I let a liberty party go ashore and they had a lot of fun climbing up that volcano. It wasn't very high, maybe a thousand feet, maybe less. The next time we went in there it was spouting all over the place. It had filled in to the mainland on the other side - looked pretty risky, apparently isn't.

I've read in the papers a good many times since of it going off. Kagashima's still there.

But the town was the most southern big city in Japan, and it was apparently the oldest city in Japan. Legend had it that that was where the Japanese first started out after coming out of the South Pacific somewhere as a race.

It was also the nearest city to Okinawa, so all the time we were bombing the Empire from Okinawa anybody that got weathered out on their target or had a few bombs left, dumped them on Kagashima on the way home, so the place was fairly well wrecked. Every wall in the place had bullet marks on it.

When they heard the Americans were coming in, the town officials told the people that they would all be raped and murdered so they might as well have a big festival first. They killed all the chickens, pigs, livestock, had a big feast, and then took to the hills.

The Marines went in and occupied a deserted city, and pretty much of a mess. They wanted labor to clean up the place, and commandeered whatever rice was around and offered food to anybody who could come and join their working party. Eventually the people in the hills got hungry and began trickling back and found they weren't murdered. They were given food and a job. And then they got mad, and the Marines were having a dickens of a time to keep them from murdering the mayor and the city fathers that had told them to take to the hills.

Mine was a rather boring job. I wanted to come home. The war was over. I didn't have any great desire to be the conquering hero. I was sort of the cop on the corner.

Q: It sounds like a big job though because you were in charge of all naval units ...

van Deurs: Yes, but there was nothing to do. I was not on the beach. The Army and the Marines had occupied the place; they had it under control.

Q: Kind of a standby job?

van Deurs: It was a standby job in case something went wrong. I was supposed to do something about it, nobody would tell me what. I didn't know whether I could start shooting or not without getting a court martial; nobody was about to tell me. As a flag officer you were on your own and it was up to you to figure out what to do in any situation.

I read everything I could find, on the Japanese, trying to figure out how they think. I thought - if this was turned around, if this was San Francisco and we were defeated, I'd sure be over there trying to think up some dirty tricks, so maybe they are. No dirty tricks ever came out of it; it was an amazing deal.

To keep from going stir crazy with nothing to do, I used to take along one of my staff. In the harbor of Sasebo, the walls go pretty near straight up, with rice terraces to the top, naval installation right at the waterfront, a lot of caves going into these hills where they had stores and so on, and on top were farms, land just anywhere around there hacked up into these rice terraces. Of course we did take the precaution of putting a pistol in the pocket, never had any occasions to use it. People were perfectly peaceful.

The crews were allowed liberty in certain restricted areas around the navy yard where the little town was. I hiked all over, into the country there with one or two of the staff. We would come to a place where there was a beautiful view, water and hills and sea and so on, "Hey, this is beautiful, something on a postcard, this is tourist stuff. Why don't I like it? It stinks, I just don't like it. I want to go home."

Q: How long before you were given a chance to leave?

van Deurs: Oh, till May I think.

Q: That would have been '46.

van Deurs: Yes. But you were just standing by in case something happened. We got the word one day from Marine Intelligence that some of the ex-Kamikaze pilots were getting together, they were going to try to raid a ship that night, one of the cargo ships we had along sice of the dock. I couldn't do anything except tell the skipper of the thing to put on the floodlights over the dock and put on some extra sentries. The only thing that happened - this gang went to a teahouse to get a lot of saki and get their nerve up and when they came out drunk enough to start the thing, they came out single file and a couple of big Marines outside hit them over the head as they walked out and threw them into the Black Maria and put them in the brig. So nothing more came of that.

The radio station at Sasebo had some six hundred foot concrete towers, with smaller antennas spread all over a hill there, besides up on the towers. It had been a forbidden bombing target. It was the main transmitter for the Japanese Fleet, and we were getting too much dope out of reading their messages ever to let anybody bomb that station, so it was completely undamaged.

Our communicators decided they wanted to take it over and put it in operation and transmit a fleet Fox schedule there. A couple of them came over to inspect it. I went down there, to the boat landing, walked up the road. There were three or four very nice little cottages. In one of them we found an ex-lieutenant who'd been the commanding officer of the place. He spoke English and was glad to show us all around the place, and it was very interesting. They even had antennas cut to all our frequencies that they'd used for jamming. They never bothered us very much, but they'd been trying.

It was very easy to patch it up and put it to work. They didn't have any power down there. The power line from Sasebo was broken. They had a big underground diesel generator, but they didn't have any oil left to run it. It took a very special kind of oil that was much lighter than our diesel oil.

Going back towards the boat, somebody remarked there wasn't any damage around, so the Marines can't have been there. All up around Sasebo everything that had been part of the military installation, some Marine had stuck a demolition charge in it and blown it up, emplacements, searchlights, and things like that - no damage around the radio station at all.

This ex-lieutenant showed us a little tea house out on the peninsula that had been Admiral Yamamoto's favorite place for contemplation. And a little Japanese boy about four years old, I guess cute little fellow, stepped out in the middle of the road in front of us, and put his hands on his hips and spouted all the English he had heard. He said, "Tojo is horse shit."

So, there had been Marines here!

That was his full supply of English.

Q: When did you leave Japan then?

van Deurs: By May I'd really finished the job, got rid of most of the ships, and there wasn't anything to do. Sherman was running the fleet by that time. I sent him word that the job was really finished, they didn't need me any more, and he ordered me on to Tokyo with the cruisers and destroyers that I had left.

I told him, "I want to be home." He couldn't understand me wanting to give up commodore's rank and go back to captain. Sherman never had given up anything - he was that kind of a man.

I finally told him, I said, "I don't get any extrapay for being a commodore, and probably pretty soon they'll cut down on the number of flag officers on flight pay. As a commodore I might get chopped off. I'd rather be a captain with flight pay than a commodore without it."

I put it that way because I knew Sherman was personally a very selfish guy. He always wanted his share of everything. So that made sense. He right away wrote a dispatch to the Bureau of Personnel saying I could be released.

Inside of a matter of hours one came back from Pearl signed "Towers," bawling hell out of Sherman for releasing an officer from the Fleet without his permission. Towers was trying to protect my commission, I think, but I didn't care.

We did not get an answer from BuPers, so Sherman signed me as a supernumerary on his staff. I came home - he was ordered home just about that time. I came home as a passenger in the IOWA.

When I got over to Tokyo that time, I had the flu, or something. I was running a high temperature. I moved into the IOWA and crawled in a bunk for about three or four days, taking aspirin and so on.

But that was a very fine trip home.

Q: You went to Alameda for a little while?

van Deurs: They gave me thirty days leave, and ordered me to command Patrol Wing Fourteen with headquarters at Alameda.

While I was on leave Ann and I drove around the Coast here, up to Yosemite, down to Monterey - I don't know where all. Somewhere along the line I picked up a letter from Moebus that said, "It's still on the Secret list, don't tell anybody, but that outfit you're going to is going to be decommissioned, and you're going to be ordered to the War College, so don't buy a house."

I went to Alameda. My old friend, John Dale Price, was the fleet air commander. They had some old quonset huts made into apartments that you could get for transient quarters - Ann and I moved into one of those.

Everybody was helpful, suggesting this, that, and the other on a place to live. They thought it was kind of funny that we were content to sit in a quonset and eat our meals over at the Club and kind of loaf around. We had friends over in the city, where we could visit in the evening a bit.

Couldn't tell anybody that I knew the thing was going out of commission, but they thought we were nuts that we weren't rushing around looking for a place to live. I think in about a month it happened, and we went to Newport to the War College there.

Q: Did you enjoy that?

van Deurs: In some ways yes, in a lot of ways no.

Q: Most of it you didn't need, did you?

van Deurs: There was a very peculiar situation. I was delighted to go because Spruance had just gone as President of the War College and I admired him so much. I thought I'd get a chance to soak up some of Spruance's know-how, it would be wonderful.

But we got there and I found that the War College during the war had been abbreviated to train Reserves for staff duty. Most of the staff of the place were second raters that had been sent there because nobody wanted them at sea, and a lot of them were held over. And while Spruance was the head man, they were running the detailed show.

It was the first class of senior officers after the war, and there were quite a few Army and Air Force people. A lot of the students had a couple of rows of battle ribbons. Most of them were specialists in one thing and another, and any time one of the staff people got up on the platform and started to lecture there were at least ten people in the audience who knew more about the subject than he ever would.

Q: That's why I say you didn't need it.

van Deurs: It made it fun because the staff was getting constantly slapped down by the students. "That isn't so, this is the way you do it," and that kind of stuff. They were still running problems on the old game board, with funny rules about air, and the staff couldn't get it through their heads - the fact that in a situation like we were in on the TENNESSEE, when there was an attack coming in, you didn't sit down and write papers. Somebody, the admiral, or whoever was the head man, had to make a decision right now - do we shoot or don't we shoot? And pull the string or get off the pot, as it were.

At the College it was all slow motion, so a lot of us kicked all the time and made ourselves rather unpopular kicking about it.

The man I relieved as Oldendorf's Chief of Staff, Rafe Bates, was down in the basement of the War College in the archives, putting together sort of an official history of the action reports of the war, a strategic analysis of them.

Rafe was a peculiar guy. He got up and put on a lecture on the Battle of Midway at one point. His manner more than anything else offended. He was talking down his nose at everybody. By the time the lecture was over everybody in the audience was just madder'n hell, all insulted.

Q: Some of them had been there, I suppose.

van Deurs: Yes, some of them had been there.

Some time later, he was scheduled to put on another lecture on some other battle out there, and up and down the corridors there was a mutiny brewing. People weren't going to take that any more. They didn't like that guy and so on. There was a lot of dirty talk.

I don't know if you know how the War College is run, but there is an auditorium and a game room, and there are a lot of study rooms where there's a desk and chairs and bookshelves and so on for two officers. You shared the room with somebody else. I had an Army colonel with me. They mixed the services that way. But in working out problems and so on there was a lot of bull throwing around the room and between rooms, and you got a lot of ideas. I talked with the other students and so on. If you didn't know about some type of work you went next door and found somebody who was an expert at it. It was kind of a free atmosphere.

There was an awful lot of reading and an awful lot of research to be done, quite a bit of paperwork, and then this mutiny was brewing over the next lecture by Bates.

I hunted him up below and told him, "I don't know whether you know it or not but you've insulted practically everybody in the place, and if you do it again tomorrow the lid's going to blow off."

He was quite taken aback, said he didn't mean anything like that. He was just trying to put out the dope as he saw it. He took my remarks very well.

He was still a commodore at that time; I'd gone back to captain's stripes. But he was man enough to think it over and change the tone, and the second lecture he got away with it. It was kind of a tough thing to do, but I remembered he'd helped me a lot when I took over, as I told you, so that worked out.

Q: Did you learn anything there that year?

van Deurs: I learned a lot from the other students, not much from the staff.

I came across a couple of theses I had to write at the place, the other day; one of them was on atomic energy, and I see no reason to change it today. So maybe we learned something.

But they only got Spruance on the platform once to talk; that was sort of by demand. The students said, "We came here to learn something from Admiral Spruance." He talked to us for quite some time about a number of things, and then threw himself open to questions, and that was a very enlightening day.

One of the questions, from one of the Army people I think, was, "When you're planning one of these big operations, how do you know how many battleships and transports and cruisers and carriers and what not you need? How do you figure how many of each you'r going to have to have to do the job?"

Spruance said, "You can't figure, you take everything you can get, and then when you're halfway there you wish you had some more."

He was a very modest man. They were giving him a lot of credit for the Battle of Midway. There'd been a couple of books published about the thing, about how he'd thought and so on. He said, "It's all wrong. I didn't do any of that. All I knew was, I had to get those other carriers before they got me. The rest of it, the talk of strategy, is all bull. That was all I was trying to do."

Q: But he still went away at the right time and came back at the right time.

van Deurs: Well, it worked.

Q: How did you get command of the PHILIPPINE SEA?

van Deurs: At the end of the year, much to my surprise, they asked me to stay on for the staff. That was the last thing I wanted. I got out of that because I had been picked in WAshington for a sea command. The College said they wouldn't stop that; anything else, why yes. I went from the War College to the PHILIPPINE SEA, that was all.

Apparently as one wise Navy wife put it that you were "being processed for admiral," that is, the ones who were given a sea command at that time were being given a chance at it. I don't know whether that was true or not.

The War College claimed they didn't put out any grades, didn't do any marking, but there was apparently a secret system because the detail officer in the Bureau of Aeronautics happened to be a friend of mine at the time and he showed me this. I was standing up at the top of the thing, and therefore I was picked for the ship.

Q: Did you enjoy that duty?

van Deurs: Very much. She was a beautiful ship and she was only a year old. I took over in Hoboken the day before she was to go to the Brooklyn Navy Yard, and spend the summer in the Brooklyn Navy Yard under overhaul.

I found a schoolteacher's apartment up on East 84th Street near the river, found a place where I could climb over the handrail of the freeway along there and hop into a boat, so I used to go to the Navy Yard in one of the little personnel boats. It was very nice - ride down the river on a sunny day reading the newspaper and watch the poor suckers fighting the traffic on the East River Drive.

Q: And of course on the PHIL SEA you didn't have anybody shooting at you.

van Deurs: No, nobody was shooting at you. You weren't sure they weren't going to, a couple of times.

We came out of the Yard in the fall and went to Quonset to pick up an air group. While in the Yard they changed all my heads of departments and most of the crew. We started green with a new air group. I think we worked out a few days off Newport, and then were sent down to Guantanamo for underway training.

Did I tell you that before?

Q: You told me that you went on underway training and you told me then about Admiral Bogan, but you didn't tell me on the tape.

van Deurs: That training at that time consisted of a crew of specialists that came aboard every morning. There was a captain leading them, and some of them were chiefs, some were enlisted men, some were lieutenants, but each one was a specialist in some part of carrier operations and some part of the machinery of the ship, and they scattered all through the ship.

We got underway and went to sea, and did whatever was on the schedule — some kind of a problem, and operated the air group, casualty drill. And at the end of the day about supper time we'd be back in Guantanamo and anchor there. Then all these observers would turn in pencil notes of what they'd seen and what was wrong in the part of the ship where they'd been working. They talked it over with me a little bit in the cabin, and then went ashore.

I sent for the heads of departments and dealt these pencil notes out and said, "Here, fix this before tomorrow, see that it goes right next time."

The trick was to make people stop alibiing. The first reaction of most people was, "That ain't so, that fellow didn't know what he was talking about." You finally got the idea across that these people were just trying to help us, there wasn't anything derogatory, but here was something that could be made better, and then it began to work fine.

That went on for ten days, two weeks. It ended up with an admiral's inspection. That was sort of the final examination. Jerry Bogan was the Commander Air Atlantic at that time. He flew down from Norfolk, and put on this inspection.

I don't know whether I mentioned it before, but Jerry was a pretty rough, tough character in a way, an excellent carrier group commander during the war, very much of a fighting Irishman, and he hated pomp and ceremony.

The first time he came aboard he waved away the side boys and said, "Don't have any of that God damned business for me."

Going ashore that afternoon, the side boys were there again, and he turned around and gave me a growl, "I really mean it, I don't want 'em." After that there were no side boys.

He just pooh-poohed ordinary ceremony. Thereby he offended a lot of black shoe people, but he'd been that way all his life, - very outspoken, said whatever he felt at anytime. He was one of the better people at it.

The ship came through his inspection very well. I was kind of flattered, as he went down the gangway the last time he said, "I don't think you've wasted a damn minute down here."

Q: Then you took off for the Mediterranean?

van Deurs: No, we went back to the States. We put into Norfolk to pick up a battalion of Marines. The government had decided to keep a Marine landing force afloat in the Mediterranean. They were sending most of their heavy equipment in a cargo ship, but the carrier was to berth both the troops and the commanding colonel. The PHILO SEA was a flagship. I guess I went back to Quonset first, picked up the admiral and messed around there for a while, and then started for the Caribbean again, but I had orders to pick up this Marine battalion. There was some kind of a fleet problem going on down in the Caribbean, had to go from there.

Ralph Jennings was the Admiral. I'd know him a long time. He was an old time flier, and I never thought too smart, and certainly wasn't a fast thinker, but perfecly nice guy.

When we got this order to go in to Norfolk, the dispatch said, "There's a colonel in command of this battalion." I asked the admiral if he was going to ask the colonel to join his mess, the flag mess. Well, Ralph didn't know; he didn't know the guy. He didn't like to have people around that he didn't know, he wasn't sure. I said, "I want my executive officer to be the senior office in the wardroom, and I thought if you weren't going to invite him to your mess I'd invite him to mess with me."

That took all the weight of decision off Ralph; that was fine.

So we took them aboard, and I sent word to this colonel that I'd be pleased if he'd join the cabin mess, just the two of us, which he did.

It turned out to be a very happy idea, because Colonel Bo Ridgeley was one of the survivors of the Death March at Bataan and quite an unusual man. He had been in the Fourth Marines at Shanghai that had moved down to Corregidor just before the shooting began, and he'd been taken prisoner. He had gone into Billibid at Manila, I think. There he volunteered for labor. (Under the Geneva Convention, which the Japanese followed, they could force enlisted prisoners to work on non-military projects, and had to pay them. An officer could volunteer for work on the same basis.)

Ridgeley volunteered and they had him marching out with a bunch of other prisoners every day into the jungle somewhere cutting wood. One reason he volunteered, he had a system where he was dropping messages on the trail without the Japanese guards seeing him that the guerillas picked up later on. They'd keep in touch with the guerillas on the outside of the prison. Also he set snares and traps in the jungle, and whatever he caught he took back to camp and threw in the rice kettle, to get more protein for the prisoners. He boasted one day that he'd eaten everything that swam or flew or crawled. He said, "I've caught snakes, birds, monkeys ..."

I said, "How does a dead Jap taste?"

He threw up his hands and said, "That's one thing I never tried, I take it back."

He said the only thing that went wrong, he got a little monkey one day that had been eating some hot peppers and threw him in the rice kettle, and it was so hot with pepper that they couldn't eat the rice.

He managed to get the rice water that they used to wash out the rice tubs after they cooked it and put it in old saki bottles that he found. He left it uncorked under the barracks and yeast grew in it. He made the other prisoners and himself drink that so they'd get some Vitamin B out of the yeast. It was a very good idea

He kept a record of everybody that died in the camp and where they were buried, without the Japs knowing it. When they finally decided to take him out of the Philippines he buried his records, and after he was sprung at the end of the war he went back and dug them up. These were the only records we ever had of a whole bunch of people.

The exec came in one day and said, "Hey, what kind of a colonel is that you've got up there? He was down in the wardroom the other night. Some of us were sitting around and the steward put a bowl of apples on the table. We all grabbed one and were munching and talking. Most people tossed the core in the ash tray, but the colon didn't toss any, he ate core and all."

I said something to him and he said, "Aw hell, it's all digestible, it just depends on how much you wanted to stay alive, you ate everything."

One night we had some little fish that had bones in it, head and tail like a trout, and when I got through the bones and head and tail were on my plate. When the colonel got through there was nothi on his plate. I said something to him about it and he said, "Oh, that makes my wife very mad, but ..." He said he got in the habit of it. "Fish bones are completely digestible."

He said he thought one reason he survived was he didn't smoke. He said a lot of the people got so desperate for tobacco that they would trade their rations for a cigarette or part of a cigarette, and a lot of them died because they'd rather have tobacco than food.

The Japanese system - if a Japanese soldier gets sick his ration stops. He doesn't get fed in the hospital unless his family brings him food. He's not working for the Emperor, and so the Emperor isn't feeding him. The same thing went for the prisoners. When they were down sick - no chow. So if you once got down sick you never got up again, so no matter how bad you felt or how much malaria you had or anything else, you had to stay on your feet and stagger around to survive.

Another one of his stories --- when we began to get close to the Philippines they began evacuating prisoners back to Japan. He was on a ship, loaded into the hold of a cargo ship. Before it got very far from Manila one of our submarines torpedoed it. The Japanese abandoned ship. The prisoners broke out of the hold. They weren't very far off Luzon. They had a cargo of sugar apparently along with prisoners. Before they went over the side to try to swim for the beach, Ridgely looked around and found a lot of Japanese canteens, filled them with sugar, strapped them on, and made the beach with that. By putting a little water with it and making the prisoner survivors drink that, he got some strength back into some of them.

He was thinking all the time. He probably weighted over two hundred pounds, a short stocky fellow, big legs, big arms, broad shoulders. I think he weighed around ninety pounds when we got him out of the prison camp in Korea. Yes, he got as far as Korea, very sick and what have you, but survived. Before they brought him home they flew him down to the Philippines to dig up those records.

He was quite a companion. The cruise was four or five months, and I enjoyed his company very much.

Q: What did the PHILO SEA do? What was its mission during that time?

van Deurs: We were first sent down to the war games, very briefly, down in the Caribbean, and then went to the Mediterranean to relieve the carrier there in the Sixth Fleet.

The first part of it, we made several French ports in Africa and the south of France. We were supposed to spend a week in Naples but we got a radio, "Get out of there in forty-eight hours because the Italians are having an election and might go Communist, and they don't want anybody to say that the American Fleet had been in there to influence the elections." So that was cut short.

Then the British moved out of Palestine and all hell broke loose there. Something went wild in Tunis just after we were there.

One day I was over on the flagship talking to Fuzz Sherman, the Fleet Commander. He showed me a flock of instructions he'd had from Washington in the past few weeks. For each he'd put circles on a chart. Everything that happened, somebody in Washington would send a message. I think the day I was over there they'd just shot an American Consul in Jerusaleum. He looked at his watch.

"Well, in about an hour I'll get one from the White House that says stand by to do something, and about an hour after that I'll get one from the Navy Department that says get ready to do something, but that'll be all."

But here's one, ""Don't get more than a day's steaming away from Naples. Be ready to go to Israel, but don't get any further away than this from some place else."

He put all these circles down.

There was one little corner of the Mediterranean down at the bottom of the Adriatic and near Crete, that we could steam around in without violating one order or another. Nobody ever cancelled any of these things. He could only wiggle around. So we spent a great deal of time in a little island port called Argostoli, on one of the Greek islands between Italy and Greece, down at the bottom of the Adriatic. My sailors began calling it their home port, we were there so many times. The British had used it in Napoleon's time -- I guess up to World War II.

They'd had a bad time there during World War II. I got to know some of the civilians on the beach. They were completely broke, had absolutely nothing. The kids were going to school in rags and barefooted in the winter time. But Marshall Plan food was coming in and feeding them. And it was the only place - it happened all over Europe, but they were the only ones that said thank you, if it wasn't for the Marshall food we would have been starving to death. They were the only people that had the decency to say thanks. That's one reason I liked them.

The Italians had rushed in there. The minute they declared war they rushed in and took these islands. They built concrete barracks and a bunch of concrete gun emplacements to fortify the harbor entrance. They were there to stay. They'd been wanting the islands for years.

The Germans came in a little bit later, and went into a little town on the other side of the harbor entrance. About the time Italy was getting shaky, the Greeks had a great hate for Italians. They didn't seem to have much feeling about Germans, but the Italians apparently had taken over and this was going to be Italian from now on, and ground the natives down, so they hated their guts.

When Italy had surrendered, the German commander across the bay called for air support. A bunch of dive bombers appeared and blasted all the Italian emplacements in town and part of the town. Under cover of that the Germans came across the bay and took over. With great glee one of the Greeks told me how on top of the harbor pier the Italians had anti-aircraft guns surrounded by barbed wire. The Germans wrapped the Italian gun crew in their own barbed wire and threw them overboard. They marched a couple hundred of them down a road towards their barracks and machine gunned them all. They wiped them out completely, and the Greeks thought it was swell, they loved

There was one thing that they showed me there, said, "There used to be a mill right here. The Germans used it for ammunition storage and it got blown up." It had an undershot water wheel. The channel for the water and the bearings for the wheel were there. It was right on the beach, a rocky beach. They lifted up a little gate and water ran out of the sea, under the wheel and ran the mill. Where does the water go? It went down a hole.

I couldn't believe that you could go on an ocean beach, a Mediterranean beach, and watch sea water run through a little channel and down a hole about ten feet from the water's edge, and the hole never got filled up. But I went back to the ship and broke out an encyclopedia, and by golly the story was in the encyclopedia.

The natives thought nothing of it. It had always been there. Apparently they'd been doing it for hundreds of years. I still don't know where it goes to, but it's a verified fact. There it was.

We went over to Crete on a cruise. I was very much interested to go through Knossos, the ruins of ancient Crete's capitol and the labyrinth.

At the other end of Crete, the mayor of the city threw an official party for us, an official dinner, and among other things when we got in there, on the table there was a lot of bottles. There was red and white wine, club soda, and orange soda. The wine glasses were tremendous tumblers. Some of the Greeks filled them up with one kind of wine, some with the other kind, and some would take half wine and fill it up with orange soda. I never saw it done before, but it was as you like it - you drank it straight or with soda pop or what have you.

In that harbor, books said - you could look down in the clear water and see the tops of the houses of a village that had been sunk in an earthquake years ago. Some of us went looking for it in a boat one day. We couldn't locate it. The water was too rough. I saw a fisherman in a boat and tried to ask him where it was. He couldn't understand English, but he had two or three big gunnysacks in the boat and he dug into them and gave us handfuls of some green things. Let us know to eat 'em. They were green almonds in the husk, and you cut them open and ate the whole darned thing. They were very good with salt. The shells hadn't hardened yet.

Q: Were there any crises while you were there? How long were you there?

van Deurs: About six months - something like that.

There were crises all the time. The Russians were talking dirty, and there was shooting in Palestine, Italy was on edge, and so on.

Things were tense enough so that I finally went to Admiral Jennings and said that I didn't want to be another PANAY. Things really were just touch and go and anything might happen any time. I said, "Unless you direct otherwise or order me not to, I'm going to arm my planes and any time they're flying they're going to be flying with loaded machine guns, loaded for bear, in case somebody attacks."

Jennings didn't say yes, wouldn't say no, so that was exactly what we did. I put her on a war footing, but nothing happened. It was just another one of those cases of being the cop on the beat. As I say, The Fleet Commander kept getting these orders from Washington, both from the White House and the Navy Department.

Q: Be ready to do something in case you had to do something?

van Deurs: Yes. Don't get too far away from here, and don't get too far away from there, stand by, we'll tell you what to do here --- but nobody ever called for any action.

So finally we were relieved and sent back to Quonset, and the KEARSARGE came out and took our place.

Q: Then you went to duty in the office of CNO.

van Deurs: On the way back Jennings pulled one on me, said, "I've been looking over the exercises for the fiscal year. Your ship has done everything except night launching of the air group, night attack, and I figured out we could steam so you could get off Quonset in the middle of the night, fly off the planes to fly to Quonset, and that would make a clean record for you, and maybe win you the Battle Efficiency Pennant or something."

I said, "These people haven't done any night flying for five months. If it was wartime I wouldn't hesitate a bit to pop them off. But I see no reason to take a chance on that when they're out of practice, just to complete a record of exercises. Unless you directly order me to I'm not going to do it."

He wouldn't order me to, so we didn't do it.

I was very much surprised after I got down to Washington by being invited back up to Newport to see them hoist the Battle Efficiency Pennant on the ship. I think that was probably more Jerry Bogan than Jennings.

Q: It would have seemed kind of a hazardous thing for no particular point gained.

van Deurs: That's how I looked at it — no point to the darned thing. We probably could have gotten away with it without any trouble, but it was sticking our neck out for nothing but somebody's idea of a record.

Q: Then you were in CNO for two years?

van Deurs: Yes. While we were down in the Mediterranean, John Dale Price became DCNO Air. He grabbed Moebus right away and said, "You're going to Washington with me," and Moebus turned around and said he wanted me for a helper, so John Dale said, "Okay." So I got the word in the Med that that was the picture and I was going to be on the team whether I liked it or not. And I was.

Q: What did you do there?

van Deurs: Well that's a good question.

Moebus's job — I've forgotten the OP number for it — was Assistant DCNO Air for Advance Planning, and he was supposed to plan naval air for the future.

What happened by the time I got there, as happens all the time in Washington, most people spent all their time answering questions instead of doing their work. People over in the Senate and the House would send over and want facts on this or that and they had to be answered within twenty-four hours. So somebody was told -- drop what you're doing and get us the answer to this thing.

The job was supposed to be Advanced Planning, but it quickly got snowed under with something that had to be done right now today.

Q: Congressional correspondence?

van Deurs: Congressional correspondence, or the Secretary or somebody up in the front office had to be briefed for this or that.

Moebus's idea was to stick me in a back room and do the things that he didn't do, because he and all the rest of the people were answering questions.

Q: He was still a captain, wasn't he?

van Deurs: No, he'd just made rear admiral.

We started out on that basis. I got a couple of helpers, one of them a Marine colonel who was very good, and the other an officer who had been working with me at Corpus Christi and two or three other places. But we soon got sucked in. After a few months the pressure got too much and we got sucked in on dishing out answers too. It was the same old rat race. But at the very start an eye-opening experience for me as Planning Officer.

Fish had brought me in on a basis of the fact that I had done planning during the war. Corpus Christi was partly my planning, and I told you the South Pacific part of it, but it was done on a different basis in the Navy Department.

About the second day I was sitting there, a chap that had been there some time came in, one of the ex-naval constructors in my class. He said, "Well, the figure is 5.2."

I said, "What do you mean, 5.2?"

"Well, we think we can get 5.2 billion this year out of Congress. That's about what they'll go for. They gave us so much last year, and we think maybe we can argue for that. So you'd better get busy and think up reasons why we need 5.2."

I said, "What will we spend it for?"

"Oh, you always find things to spend money on. The idea is to get the money. Never mind ..."

I said, "Well, gee, somebody ought to be able to figure out what it's going to cost to do this, that, and the other thing around here."

"Oh no, you figure out reasons for 5.2."

Q: Who was this who was saying the 52.?

van Deurs: A classmate of mine.

Q: What was his job?

van Deurs: I don't know, I've forgotten now. He was round there, mostly bootlicking to make admiral, and he did it successfully.

But it sort of iritated me; I never had believed in that kind of planning.

Q: That's really bad staff work, isn't it.

van Deurs: After a couple of years around there I found that was exactly how it was done in Washington, every Department the same thing. It was just a mad scramble for money, and after you'd gotten the money then you figured out how far you could go with it. But it seemed to me backwards, that there ought to be some way to figure out what was necessary for Defense and go and ask for that. But instead you wrote all kinds of fancy worded discourses to explain the things that were urgent and terrible and terrific.

The same bird began using a lot of strange words, which I called "Pentagonese." For a while I kept a little list of them in my drawer, the cockeyed language that went around Washington. Then I found I was talking it myself, there was no way to escape. Mostly it was big words with little meanings to replace common English. After I retired, I went back to college to learn how to write without them.

But I suppose there was a broadening experience somewhere in the middle of it. I told people, I used to believe in the Great White Father, and if I ever got an order from the Navy Department I figured there was a lot of clever thinking and brainwork behind it, but now I knew the truth. They'd better not send me back to sea, because if any orders came from the Department to me I'd look at them sideways and consider them very carefully before I acted on them - view them with suspicion.

Q: This is the duty that you say disillusioned you.

van Deurs: Yes. I'd have been a much happier old man if I'd never been sentenced to the Pentagon.

Q: I had a tour of duty in the Pentagon with the Secretary of Defense, Anna Rosenberg headed it. I went through not as long but as disturbing an experience, for me.

van Deurs: This thing was at a bad time. The Air Force was riding high. The B-32 argument, or B-36 arguement, was on. Johnson was Secretary of Defence, and I always thought probably a crook. Certainly he was a pretty poor Secretary.

Q: The infighting between the services was pretty horrible.

van Deurs: It was not only horrible, but it was senseless as that 5.2 business. It had very little basis on fact.

The idea was to find ways to make the other fellow look bad and thereby get some more money. It was all part of the same picture. A great many operators, particularly in the Air Force, never let the truth interfere with a good story. So it was all a pretty replusive sort of a deal. Being an admiral in the Pentagon was just below a messenger boy. The hired help knocked off at four-thirty, captains sometimes got out of there at six, but the admirals couldn't get loose till eight or nine. It seemed to me a horrible future.

Fish said, "I'll make you an admiral, you spend a lot of time around the front office, get known around here."

I said, "No, thank you. If I have to do that to become an admiral, I'll retire otherwise."

So that's what happened.

Q: But you had your year in Europe, which you enjoyed.

van Deurs: That came about, as Ann told you ----

John Dale Price's wife asked Ann where she wanted to go, and I said, "California" and Ann said, "Europe," and so she said, "I'll tell Johnny to send Van to Europe."

We had a sort of a two faced staff or double staff in London at the time. The admiral there with the title of Commander-in-Chief Eastern Atlantic and Mediterranean had a chief of staff and the regular operating staff, but in the back room there was another chief of staff and a completely separate staff that had some Army and Air Force people on it. It was a planning staff. NATO hadn't been agreed upon yet, and this staff was charged with figuring out what we and the British could do in case the Russians moved before NATO was effective. They were talking about setting up NATO. So that was headed up by Joe Bolger, whom I mentioned earlier, and Joe allowed he'd be glad to have me on the team, so that's where I went.

But it turned into rather a frustrating experience, because the Army members mostly, and to some extent the Air Force members, were not interested in a serious plan. It was something like what happened before Pearl Harbor. (I told you about Ryan saying that it would be a nice joint exercise, but we haven't got time for it.)

The Army boys in London were trying to use any plans as a lever for the War Department to demand more money, more troops, and more equipment. What the Navy was trying to do was to figure out what we could do with what we had in case the lid blew off. But the other two services weren't interested in that, they were interested purely in using this thing as a political weapon, so that while there was a lot of planning and a lot of cross talk, very little was accomplished.

London was a lot of fun. Cat Brown was there, with an office in the same building, with the job of running the military assistance groups. He was deputy to some Army general that was heading up that operation. He got there a couple of months ahead of us. We'd been friends from way back. Ann and Elinor had a lot of fun together and so did Cat and I.

Then the Army general over in Germany said the War Department regulations required him to inspect any outfit that had Army troops in it, and all these MAAGS around Europe had Army personnel, but they had people from the other two services. If he sent an inspector around and anything was wrong, the Army would say, "Oh, the Air Force and the Navy did that." It would be ineffective. He proposed a joint inspection team. Everybody said that was fine. Admiral Connoly said that was fine, he'd ask Washington to send a captain. Washington said, "You send a captain," and they went back and forth for a month maybe, "You do it," "No, you do it, I haven't got one," "Neither have I," and so on.

Finally the admiral was down in the Mediterranean and it was getting close to a deadline. He got a message from Washington, "Have a captain over to Heidleberg by Monday morning," and so Friday afternoon, after I'd left the office a dispatch came in ordering a classmate of mine on the same staff to go to Heidelberg.

Joe Bolger called up, "Ted just got these orders and he's crying his eyes out. He's got a sick wife, children in school, a lease on an apartment. Will you take his place?"

I said, "Well, I have an apartment too, a lease on one I can't break." He said, "Well, I'm tired of living out in the country, don't want to spend another winter out there, I'll take over your apartment."

He mentioned that the Air Force was providing the transportation and I said, "I don't believe they're safe, don't believe in these airplanes. If I could drive my own car I might think about it." "Well, we'll write your orders that way." So I agreed.

I think Joe and I were supposed to go down to Malta the next morning for a conference with the British down there. So it was arranged that the other chap would go to Heidelberg, we'd go to Malta and finish that job, and as soon as we got back I'd go over to Europe and relieve him.

The Malta show was kind of funny. They wanted us to get together with the British planners from Egypt, Alexandria, but they didn't want it in the newspapers. So we landed at Malta, flew down there and landed at Malta, went to the hotel, and it was leaked out that we'd come down to see some British Fleet maneuvers. The next morning we went aboard a British cruiser in the little harbor on one side of Malta, got underway and went to sea. We were served sherry and bouillon, with easy chairs on the quarterdeck. We steamed around the other side of Malta into Valetta Harbor, and went ashore in one of the old castles there and got down to the planning business. It was good cover, and apparently it worked.

When we got back Ann and I got in our car and drove over to Brussels. Under the Army inspection system, we spent a week in each one of the capitals where they had a MAAG, going through the thing. Then we had to sit down with the commanding officer of the MAAG and tell him everything that we had thought was wrong, in a diplomatic way. Then we had to get back to Heldelberg and write up a report. The report couldn't contain anything that hadn't been mentioned in the conference, although it just had to be mentioned, it didn't have to be put the same way in the report. Under the Army system the people being inspected never got a look at the report It seemed to me that it made a difference who the commanding officer was, what went into the report. The inspector general insisted ther would be nothing derogatory about any commander that was the least bit senior to him. But it there was an Army commander a little bit junior to him, it didn't have anything good in it. What we'd seen didn't seem to have much connection with it. He didn't like a good report for either an Air Force or a Navy commander.

Well, there wasn't too much wrong, in most places. What there was wrong was on the political side of the thing, which we were ordered not to mention or touch. It was a purely military inspectio

I objected to some of the things that were put in.

It finally was agreed that there would be several reports — that I would write a report on the Navy part of it, the Air Force man would write one on his service, the Army man write one on the Army, and then there was a general report that covered the whole thing that the three of us would sign. The Navy report was sent through the senior naval officers, whoever they were, for comment, before it went to the Navy Department. I had a free hand in writing that by myself. A couple of the general reports I refused to sign, because they didn't jibe with what I'd seen. I don't know what ever happened to them.

The two colonels with us were kind of jealous. "Gee, you know you're going to retire, and you can afford to be an honest man, but I've got to keep on working for this guy. I wish I could do what you're doing." But they were very pleasant people.

Of course the reason for insisting on driving my car was so Ann could go along. She wanted to go and I couldn't afford to take her if I was paying her way all over Europe, but she could ride in the car without taking any more gasoline. So we'd leave Heidleberg on a Friday afternoon and drive to the next inspection place, and the other two birds would arrive on Monday by air, and we'd go to work. Almost every place we went there was some Navy man and his wife that we'd known before — usually the commanding admiral or the senior one under somebody else. So it was kind of an old home week, in a lot of ways.

Q: It was a pleasant last tour, wasn't it?

van Deurs: It was a very nice tour, except for my minor arguments with the inspector general.

Q: It was actually in effect your last tour, wasn't it, because when you went back to CNO ...

van Deurs: What happened there — we got back to London I guess in February. You had an option of retiring on station or going home to retire, and it seemed smart to get a good physical examination before you retired because once the papers went through there was no way to change them if there was something physically wrong.

So I wrote a letter and asked to be ordered home in time to go to Bethesda for a thorough checkup before the 30th of June.

My dumb classmate who had refused the European tour saw this, "What did you write that for?" I explained. "Well, that sounds like a good idea, I'll write one too."

Joe was relieved about that time so all three of us came home on the same transport, sharing a mess table with Admiral Pug Ainsworth, who had run the cruises down in the South Pacific. He was retired and he'd been visiting family in Europe, so it was a very pleasant trip home, except that we sat around the table daring each other to have another piece of pie, and we all got off the ship overweight.

They ordered me down to CNO — I never did any work there that time, just to check in there — and was ordered over to Bethesda for a week.

When I came back officially I was working for an old friend, Duckworth, but I had two or three weeks to go. Duckie didn't care whether I went to the office or not. I'd go once a week to see if there was any mail, that was all.

Q: You retired then June 30th, 1951.

van Deurs: Bethesda was kind of funny. I thought it was a very good system they turned us in out there. A commander, I think it was, came in to make up a medical history. We sat there and talked for an hour or so, all the injuries or symptoms you'd had during your career, anything I thought was wrong or was worried about at the time. Got a pretty good history on the thing. And then on the basis of that conversation he laid out a series of tests, examinations, and laboratory work that took a week or ten days to work through. You started out early in the morning with a schedule, go through these things, and then about four o'clock in the afternoon got back to the room.

My classmate Ted was across the corridor doing the same thing. Every afternoon he'd come in, "What did they do to you today?"

"Well, they did so and so."

"Oh gee, they didn't give me that."

"Well, they didn't think it was necessary in your case."

One day they gave me an examination that was uncomfortable and repulsive and undignified and everything else, and when Ted came in with his usual question, he said, "They never gave me that. What they ought to have around here is a checkoff list, give everybody all these things ..."

I said, "If anybody ever did to me what they did to me this afternoon because it was on a checkoff list, I'd have killed the son-of-a-bitch."

He thought that one over and decided maybe the checkoff list wasn't such a good idea after all. That was the end of it.

Q: But they found you in good health?

van Deurs: They couldn't find anything that was worth retiring me for.

Q: I wanted to ask you a question last night when we were talking, and I don't know if you want to put in on the tape, about President Kennedy, PT-109.

van Deurs: Well that's pure heresay, I wasn't there.. But Allan Calvert was commanding those PT boats at the time, and he always insisted that Kennedy's boat was cut down because he disobeyed order and that he gave him a medal, recommended him for a medal, for saving his crew, and for a general court martial for disobeying his orders. And when this author was writing PT-109 and so on, two or three people came to interview Allan - he's dead now - but that was his story and he stuck to it, but none of them dared use it.

Q: Were you going to tell me a story about the Spragues - you say they were brothers?

van Deurs: Tommy and Ziggy Sprague were both aviators. They were both in the class of '18.

Q: They were not related?

van Deurs: They were not related.

Ziggy always looked like — oh, he looked like a little old man when he was a midshipman. He had a small wrinkled face, like a little monkey's face, and a very keen sense of humor.

Tommy Sprague when he retired looked like he was in his thirties, smooth face and dark hair. He never changed.

I knew both of them through the years. At Leyte Gulf the one with the monkey face, Ziggy, was commanding the northern group that got the brunt of the shells and so on from the Japanese battleships. Tommy Sprague was commanding the division I was in, and also commanding all of the jeep carriers at Leyte.

But it was an old joke — people were always asking if they were related, and Ziggy, the one that looked like an old man, said, "No, we're not related, we're classmates, but I always introduce Tommy as my father. It makes him mad."

Q: Well I guess that pretty well brings us to the end of the biography of your career, Admiral.

van Deurs: Yes, you've got most of it.

Q: If you think of anything else I know you'll add it to the manuscript when you get it. I enjoyed it thoroughly. I hope you found it pleasant.

van Deurs: Of course we left out all the wine, women, and song, but that isn't history, that was fun.

Q: You can put that in in an addendum.

But I enjoyed it very much, and I've enjoyed being with you and Mrs. van Deurs very much.

van Deurs: Thank you. Enjoyed having you.

van Deurs: As a summary I would like to say I have always been a pacifist. I believe the same was true of many naval officers of my time. During World War I, I was one of many who believed that if this country had been ready for war, "preparededness" was the word then, the Kaiser would never have egged us into war by violating what we insisted were our rights on the high seas. Hence I wanted to make our Navy strong, strong enough so we could never be suckered into another great war.

I worked hard at, and inspite of a few rough spots, enjoyed all the jobs the Navy handed me. I loved machinery, building, testing, and trying to improve operating methods. I loved the sea, especially in its wilder moods, and above all I loved to fly. In all of my work I believed I was helping to build the strength that would preserve America's peace.

Pearl Harbor showed that strength was necessary, but was not enough by itself. We were strong, but we were attacked anyway. Politicians, not military men, brought on World War II and suckered us into it.

When we were in, like most "trade-school-boys" I did a professional job as a warrior, or wrecker. I had been trained and paid to do that if required. In smashing the enemy I was merely earning the retainer pay I had collected through the years of pleasant work. But I did not have to like that part of my job. War's wastage seemed senseless. In a few moments a skyful of bursting shells and falling planes threw away the millions of man hours spent in making that ammunition and those planes. Some smashed cities might be classed as needed slum-clearance, or making room for factory modernization, but the accompanying losses of irreplacable ancient art and history were repulsive to me. Worst of all was the death of so many fine young men and the brutalizaing of so many survivors.

At the end of World War II we hoped to relax as the world's most powerful nation. I am sure that most of those who earned battle stars wanted only peace. If the youthful theory that had guided my life was sound we should have it. Apparently I was wrong from the beginning, because for nearly twenty years there has been no peace for the United States.

I would like to believe 1970's anti-war protestors with their "stop-the-war-now" signs, broken windows, and burned buildings had a surer way to guarantee peace, but I have not heard of it yet.

INDEX

to

Interview with

Rear Admiral George van Deurs

U. S. Navy (Retired)

VOLUME II

RADM van Deurs

ACORN - an air base unit: - 449.

USS APPLACHIAN: Becomes flagship for Adm. Oldendorf in Japan, p 564.

ARGOSTOLI: Port in the Aegean Sea - used at one time by CV PHILIPPINE SEA and other units of the 6th fleet, p 592-5.

BATES, Lt. Comdr. Chester - USNR: p 446-9; sent to the U. S to form an ACORN (Air Base Unit), p 449; returns with new unit to South Pacific, p 451; called to take command of air strips on Bougainville, p 452-4; p 504.

BATES, Captain Rafe: Chief of Staff to Adm. Oldendorf - relieved by van Deurs, p 527; p 529-30; ordered to PT boats in Philippines, p 530; p 532; at the Naval War College, p 580-2.

BELLINGER, VADM Patrick N.: In command of NAS, Norfolk, 1938 - p 337-8; p 341, p 344, p 347; Adm. Kimmel asks him to work out compromise with Air Force on defense of Pearl Harbor, p 363; gets the Air Force general to sign a compromise agreement on the defense of Pearl Harbor, p 365-6.

BERNHARD, VADM Alva D.: Commandant, NAS, Corpus Christi, p 373.

BLACK CATS: Catalina amphibians based on Guadalcanal - specially trained for night work and barge hunting, p 421-2.

BLOCK, ADM Claude C.: Commandant, 14th Naval District, p 363; p 366.

BOGAN, VADM Gerald Francis: p 586; p 596.

BOUGAINVILLE: p 416; plans for airstrips on the island, p 420;

-1-

p 430.

BRISTOL, VADM Arthur L.: p 354.

BROWN, ADM Charles R. (Cat): Ran the MAAG's from London, p 603.

BROWNING, RADM Miles R.: Intelligence Officer for Adm. Halsey (1941) - on committee planning for the defense of Pearl Harbor, p 361-2; p 364; p 367-8.

CARNEY, ADM Robert B.: p 454-5; p 471.

USS CHENANGO - CVE: converted tanker; van Deurs given command (1944), p 451; p 472-7; Moratai operation - formations, p 479-80; operated as unit of 7th fleet for Moratai and Leyte operations, p 486-7; missed Leyte Gulf Battle - in Moratai picking up spare planes, p 493; object of Kamikaze search in Leyte Gulf, p 495; repairs on Bremerton and then back to fight, p 498-500; mission to the Solomons to bring a convoy of Marines for Okinawa assault, p 501; role in Okinawa campaign, p 509; p 512; plane lands by accident first day at Kadena airport, p 512-3; with carrier division relieved British at Sakishima, p 513; around the clock operations, p 515; accident and fire on board, p 515-520; continued on duty for additional sixty-six days after accident p 521; van Deurs turns over to Felt, new skipper - ordered to report to Oldendorf, p 522-3.

CINC EAST ATLANTIC and Med: van Deurs to London on the planning staff, p 602-3.

ComAirSOLOMONS: p 426-8; siege nature of Japanese attacks on base in Bougainville, p 430; planning procedures, p 436.

RADM van Deurs

COM AIR SO PAC: p 400 ff; Van Deurs makes up chart of U. S. plane capabilities, p 408-9.

DAVIS, ADM Arthur C.: Chief of Staff to Adm. Spruance on board the BB NEW MEXICO, p 523; p 526; p 536; comes int Buckner Bay with his carriers just as typhoon warnings are posted - confers with van Deurs, Chief of Staff to Oldendorf, p 551-2.

DCNO for Air (Deputy Chief of Naval Operations for Air): John Dale Price asks for Moebus and van Deurs on his staff, p 597-8; van Deurs involved in advance planning, p 598-9; van Deurs disillusioned by what went for planning, p 600.

DeFONEY, Dr.: staff doctor on Halsey Staff in Espiritu Santo, p 427-9; p 449-50.

DRAIM, Capt. Nicholas A.: p 338; Assistant Repair Officer, NAS, Norfolk, p 339; visit by van Deurs in 1942 - finds situation in shops somewhat changed because of DRAIM, p 345.

DUERFELDT, RADM Clifford (Dutch): Operations officer at Corpus Christi, p 375; p 380-1.

EKSTROM, VADM Clarence E.: (Swede) provides transportation for van Deurs and Moebus to the U. S., p 445-6; p 472.

ESPIRITU SANTO: p 404-7.

FAHRION, ADM Frank Geo.: relieves Adm. Oldendorf - sends van Deurs to Sasebo and John Tom Bottom back to Nagoya, p 570.

FELT, ADM C. D.: takes over from van Deurs as skipper of the USS CHENANGO, p 522.

RADM van Deurs

FICK, RADM Harold F.: Head of Training Department, NAS Corpus Christi, p 372-3; p 376; goes to Pensacola as Chief of Staff to Intermediate Training Command, p 376-7; places restrictions on contingent of WAVES an NAS, Corpus Christi, p 382-3; p 391.

FIFE, ADM James: the problem with U. S. Night Bombers attacking U. S. Subs on the surface in area of Rabaul, p 424.

FITCH, ADM Aubrey R.: ComAir South Pacific under Halsey - asks for van Deurs on his staff, p 400-2; p 405; p 417, p 419; moves his staff to Guadalcanal - van Deurs becomes his Chief of Staff, p 427; sends van Deurs to straighten out a base commander fracas on Vella Lavella, p 429; ordered back to Washington before South Pacific campaign is ended p 435-6; his ability to get a consensus, p 437-8 his routine on Guadalcanal, p 438-40; p 441; asks Moebus and van Deurs what assignments they want after Solomons, p 444; p 451; p 464; p 506; p 527.

USS FRANKLIN - CV: Repairs in Bremerton, p 498; p 507-8.

FRENCH FRIGATE SHOALS: Use of by U. S. patrol planes, p 348; p 350-1.

GATES, The Hon. Thomas: Assistant Secretary of the Navy for Air, p 392-3.

GEHRES, Captain Les: skipper of the FRANKLIN at time of Kamakaze attack, p 508.

GEIGER, General Ray Stanley, USMC: Commanding First Marines for Assault on Okanawa, p 503.

GREEN ISLAND: p 430-1.

GUADALCANAL: p 407-8; advanced base for Adm. Halsey, p 419, p 422; p 444; p 501; the island revisited six months later, p 502-3; p 506.

HALMAHERA: p 481; rescue operation of pilot in Halmahera lagoon, p 482-3; boost in morale of pilots, p 484.

HALSEY, Fleet Admiral Wm. F.: p 410; his attitude towards Munda operation, p 411, p 415; his headquarters on Noumea, p 419; advance headquarters on Guadalcanal, p 419; changes plans for naval activities in the SLOT, p 421; p 436-7; p 454; his personal leadership ability, p 465; visit to Guadalcanal while still under Japanese fire, p 466-9; suggests that the over-all plan of the war be altered, p 485; room for misinterpretation of battle damage reports of Sherman and others out of San Bernadino Strait, p 491-2; p 505-6.

INTERMEDIATE TRAINING COMMAND: included both Pensacola and Corpus Christi, p 376 ff.

JAPANESE SURRENDER: U. S. precautionary positioning of Oldendorf's Task Force outside Tokyo Bay p 560-1.

JENNINGS, ADM Ralph E.: in command of carriers in the Mediterranean, p 587; p 595.

USS JOHNSON - DD: Lost in Battle of Leyte Gulf, p 495.

JOHNSTON ISLAND: used in war games (1939), p 355-6.

KAMIKAZE - attacks; p 500; p 536.

KAVIENG: combined attack on the harbor, p 425-6; p 460.

KERAMA RETTO: p 514.

KESSING, RADM Oliver O. (Scrappy): Base commander at Ulithi, p 504; at Subic Bay, p 504-5.

KETCHAM, VADM Dixwell; (Dixie): p 474; p 476.

KIMMEL, RADM Husband E.: asks for additional patrol planes and crews, p 360; sends Bellinger and van Deurs for conversations with Air Force General at Fort Shafter - to work out compromise in defense of Pearl Harbor, p 363-4; p 367.

KINKAID, ADM Thomas C.: p 455; p 482; p 488-9; p 492; p 496.

LEYTE GULF: Plan put into operation after Moratai and Halsey's recommendation that schedule to speeded, p 486-9; knowledge of Japanese fleet intentions, p 489; Oldendorf sent to meet units in Surigao Strait, p 489; engagement in San Bernadino Strait, p 489-92; surprise appearance of Japanese BB's p 492-3; p 496.

LONGQUIST, Lt. Comdr. Ted: Repair officer at Norfolk NAS (1938), p 337-8; p 344.

MAAG: p 603; van Deurs on inspection trip in Western Europe; p 605-6.

MacARTHUR, General Douglas: p 455; gives a dinner for Adm Nimitz in Brisbane hotel, p 455-8; method of obtaining news stories from his communiques, p 459-60; agrees to speed-up in invasion of Philippines, p 485-6; his insistence that units of 7th fleet are under his command, p 487; resultant difficulties with Kinkaid to Halsey messages, p 487-8.

U. S. MARINES: on Guadalcanal, p 443-4.

McCAIN, ADM John Sydney: 398.

MITSCHER, ADM Marc Andrew: p 409; how he operated as Com
   Air Solomons, p 418.

MOEBUS, VADM Lucian Ancel (Fish):   Brother in law to van Deurs,
   p 397-8; goes to South Pacific as Chief of Staff to Adm
   Fitch, p 400; p 402; p 414; becomes Chief of Staff to
   Com Air Solomons, p 427-8; his quarters on Bougainville,
   p 430-2; leave in Sydney, p 441; p 444; p 449; p 451;
   521-2; p 578; on staff of DCNO for Air, p 597.

MOELLER, CMDR. Lou, CEC: Officer in charge of construction
   at NAS, Corpus Christi (1941), p 373-4.

MONTGOMERY, VADM A. E.:   Takes command of NAS, Corpus Christi,
   p 376-8; his attitude towards WAVES on the station, p 383-4;
   offers van Deurs job as Chief of Staff, p 400.

MORATAI Operation: p 479-81; Halsey suggests the war schedule
   be speeded up as result of Moratai and bombing efforts
   in Philippines, p 485.

MUNDA Operation: p 410-12; Com Air Solomons moves base to
   Munda, p 426; p 463.

NAGASAKI: Conditions there when U. S. troops landed, p 561-3.

NAVAL AIR STATION, Corpus Christi: van Deurs reports as
   Assistant Superintendent, Aviation Training (Aug. 1941),
   p 372-3; van Deurs becomes aviator consultant to the
   officer in charge of construction, p 373-4; manner in
   which practice bombing site was obtained, p 374-5; van
   Deurs becomes Superintendent of Aviation Training after

RADM van Deurs

Fick goes to Pensacola, p 377; Corpus becomes a training center with satellite commands, p 377-8; statistics on peak training period, p 378-9; accidents in Training, p 381; WAVES comes to the Air Station, p 382-4; manner in which expansions were absorbed, p 387-8; story on the authorization of auxilliary facilities at Beaville, p 392-4; van Deurs leaves for the Pacific, p 400-1.

NAVAL AIR STATION - Norfolk: June, 1938 - van Deurs becomes Structural Overhaul Superintendent and Test Pilot - p 335-346; problems with labor, p 337-342; changes in the station by 1942, p 345.

U. S. NAVAL WAR COLLEGE: van Deurs ordered there from Alameda, p 578-583.

NEW GEORGIA: p 412-3.

NIMITZ, Fleet Admiral Chester W.: guest of MacArthur at dinner, p 455-7; agrees with Halsey recommendation that invasion of Leyte Gulf be undertaken, p 485; calls Oldendorf to Guam conference after Hiroshima, p 538-9.

OKINAWA: USS CHENANGO acts as escort for the First Marines - leaving Guadalcanal for Okinawa, p 501; p 509; Oldendorf's role at Okinawa, p 534-6; Oldendorf changes flagships in Buckner Bay, p 540; typhoon heads for island, p 550 ff; results of this storm, p 554-5.

OLDENDORF, ADM Jesse B.: in command of old BB's in Battle of Surigao Strait, p 489; p 492; p 496-7; van Deurs ordered as his Chief of Staff, p 522-3; van Deurs reports to him on BB TENNESSEE, p 526-7; account of his accident at Ulithi, p 527-8; his calm attitude under fire, p 529; not an idea man, p 531; p 532; call on Spruance, p 532-3; nature of his command at Okinawa, p 534-5; after Okinawa his mission to protect U. S. minesweepers as they cleared China Sea to Vladisvostok, p 537-8; called to Guam for conference after Hiroshima, p 538-9; injured by the torpedo explosion on BB PENNSYLVANIA, p 544; flies to Japan to check on prisoner of war releases, p 549-50; unable to return to command because of typhoon, p 550 ff; in command of special Task Force that stood guard outside Tokyo Bay during surrender ceremony, p 560-1; plans relaxed trip to the U. S. after landing troops in Japan, p 564; ordered to remain in Japan, p 564-5; p 568; ordered to dissolve staff in Japan, p 569-70.

PAINTER, Comdr. Bill: (USNR): Sea Bee - on Adm. Fitch's staff, p 412-3; his mission to survey possible sites for an air strip on New Georgia, p 413; designated as the officer in charge of construction on the Segi Plantation, p 414-16.

PATROL SQUADRON 23: van Deurs takes command in Hawaii - March, 1939, p 348-9; van Deurs undertakes preparations for conflict, p 352-6; preparations to operate from Wake Island, p 357; average patrol from Pearl Harbor, p 357-8; development of bases at Midway, Wake, Johnston and Canton, p 358; Adm. Richardson institutes a stepped-up program of reconnaissance out of Pearl Harbor, p 359-60; Kimmel request for planes and crews, p 360.

PEARL HARBOR - Defense plans: see entries under BELLINGER, KIMMEL, MILES BROWNING.

PEARL HARBOR DAY: Recollections, p 385-6.

USS PENNSYLVANIA - BB: Sails to Buckner Bay to become flagship of Adm. Oldendorf, p 540-1; description of the interior, p 541; ship torpedoed, p 542-5; account of the action, 546; after Bremerton repairs she became a target ship at Bikini tests, p 547-8.

PENSACOLA: Becomes center for Intermediate Training Command, p 376; p 386; p 388; p 394.

USS PHILIPPINE SEA - CV: van Deurs takes command of her, p 583-4; a new air group and new department heads, p 585; training at Guantanamo, p 585; inspection by Adm. Bogan - p 586; in the Mediterranean, p 591; - p 595; wins the battle efficiency pennant, p 596.

PRICE, ADM John Dale: p 549-50; p 578; becomes DCNO for Air - takes Moebus and van Deurs on his staff, p 597; sends van Deurs to London, p 602.

USS PRINCETON: Under command of Adm. Sherman - lost in Battle of San Bernadino Strait, p 490-2.

PRISONERS OF WAR - Evacuation: Adm. Oldendorf goes to Japan to see about release of prisoners of war, p 549; ships sent from Okinawa to embark the prisoners, p 558-9.

RABAUL: Objective of U. S. Forces as they worked up from Guadalcanal, p 410; Roger Simpson's raid on the harbor, p 425-6.

RADM van Deurs

RADFORD, ADM Arthur: Director of Training in Washington at time of Pearl Harbor, p 386-7.

RAMSEY, VADM Paul H.: with patrol squadron 23 at Pearl Harbor (1939), p 349-50.

REIFSNIDER, VAD, Lawrence: commanding the amphibious forces enroute from Guadalcanal to Okinawa, p 502.

RICHARDSON, ADM James Otto: attempts to step up patrol schedules out of Pearl Harbor, 1940-41; p 359; names committees to consider different aspects of defense of Pearl Harbor, p 361-2; p 367.

RIDGELEY, Col. Bo: Command of battalion of Marines on the PHILIPPINE SEA, p 587-8; his recollections of prison under the Japanese, p 588-591.

ROOSEVELT, The Hon. Franklin D.: p 367.

ROYAL NEW ZEALAND AIRFORCE: p 433-4.

RUSSELL ISLANDS: p 461-3.

USS ST. LO - CVE: Sunk in Leyte Gulf Operation, p 495, p 497.

SAKISHIMA GUNTO: p 513.

SALLADA, ADM Harold B. (Slats): detail officer in Washington (1938), p 340, p 342-3.

SAMPLE, RADM Wm. D.: Admiral in command of two-carrier escort from Guadalcanal to Okinawa, p 501-3; 514; p 522.

SAN BERNADINO STRAIT: p 489-92; see also entry under Halsey.

USS SANGAMON: flagship of Admiral Sample, p 503.

USS SARATOGA - CV: Fish Moebus given command, p 451; p 521.

SASEBO: van Deurs ordered to take over duties there in place of Fahrion, p 571-2; p 574-5; radio station there for Japanese fleet communications - not a bombing target for U. S. Planes, p 576-7.

SHERMAN, ADM Forrest Percival: Operations officer for Adm. Nimitz (1945) - on the atom bomb, p 539-40.

SHERMAN, ADM Frederick Carl: (Ted) At San Bernadino Strait, p 490; his attitude towards claims of enemy losses, p 490-1; impression given that Japanese were defeated and heading back to Manila, p 490-1.

SIMPSON, RADM Rodger Whitten: p 425-6.

SOLOMON ISLANDS: Operations in the islands, p 400 ff; June 1944 decision made to close the operation, p 444.

SPECHT, RADM Wm. C.: in command of PT boats operating from Florida Island, p 422.

SPRAGUE, ADM Thomas L.: in command of carrier division, p 474; p 481-2; p 484; p 493-4; p 501; p 609-610.

SPRUANCE, ADM Raymond: p 470; van Deurs pays a call in midst of the Battle for Okinawa, p 524; joins the Admiral's party for mess, p 525-6; p 532; according to Oldendorf the stories Sprauance told were intended to convey his orders, p 533; p 564-5; p 569; President of the Naval War College, p 579-80; p 582; his comments on Midway, p 583.

STREET, Colonel: Air Force officer on planning committee with Miles Browning for defense of Pearl Harbor, p 362-3.

SYDNEY, Australia: R and R in Sydney, p 442.

RADM van Deurs

USS TENNESSEE - BB: flagship of Oldendorf - van Deurs reports, p 526-7; p 534; p 536; part of Oldendorf's Task Force to guard mine sweepers in China Sea, p 537; Oldendorf changes flagship in Buckner Bay, p 540; Oldendorf moves his flag back to TENNESSEE after the PENNSYLVANIA was torpedoed, p 547; Oldendorf goes up to Japan on prisoner of war mission - leaves command with Chief of Staff, p 549-50; typhoon warning p 550 ff; van Deurs takes fleet out of harbor to escape storm, p 553 ff; p 563-4.

TOKYO: condition of city when U. S. troops entered, p 566.

TOMLINSON, 'Indian Joe': Chief of Staff to Chief of Primary Training in Kansas City, p 387.

TOWERS, ADM John Henry: Assists van Deurs to leave NAS, Norfolk for assignment in Honolulu, p 343; sends van Deurs to Corpus Christi - duty as Assistant Superintendent of Aviation Training, p 371; takes over from Adm. Spruance, p 569; p 570-1; p 578.

TROOP LANDINGS - Japan: after the surrender, p 560-3; p 568-9; in Kagashima, p 573.

TURNER, ADM R. Kelly: notes on his planning methods. p 509-11.

TYPHOON: approaches Okinawa, p 550-3; most fleet units get out of Buckner Bay into the China Sea to ride out storm, 554; the story of the U. S. Coast Guard patrol boat, 559-60; a second typhoon, p 564.

ULITHI: p 504; assembly point for assault on Okinawa, p 507.

van Deurs, RADM George: falls victim of malaria on Espiritu Santo, p 427-8; promoted to Commodore when he reports to

Admiral Oldendorf, p 527; re-named as Commodore when he takes over command of naval base at Sasebo, p 571-5.

WALDRON, COMDR. John Charles: Assistant in Air Plot on CV SARATOGA - convinced of the effectiveness of aircraft in combat, p 369-70; led Torpedo Squadron 8 at Battle of Midway - lost his life, p 370.

WAVES: At NAS, Corpus Christi, p 382-5.

www.ingramcontent.com/pod-product-compliance
Lightning Source LLC
Chambersburg PA
CBHW082200070526
44585CB00020B/2211